Step-by-Step

COOKBOOK

Step-by-Step
COOKBOOK

Hilary Biller
Photography by John Peacock

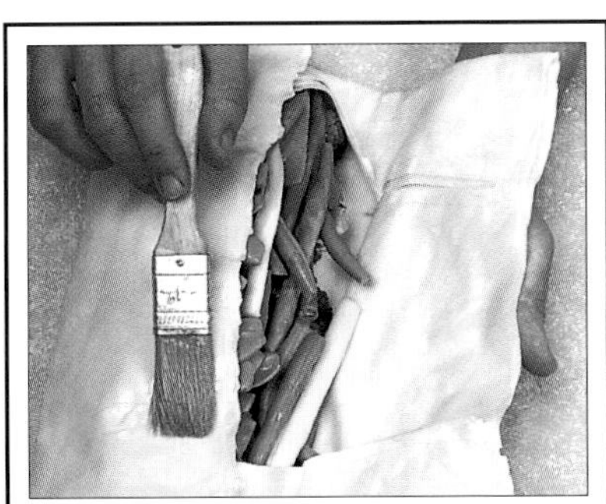

NH
NEW
HOLLAND

First published in 1995 by New Holland (Publishers) Ltd
Chapel House, 24 Nutford Place, London W1H 6DQ

ISBN 1 85368 352 3

Editor Sally Dicey
Design Director Janice Evans
Designer Suzanne Fortescue
Cover Designers Janice Evans and Suzanne Fortescue
Design Assistant Lellyn Creamer
Photographer John Peacock
Food Stylists Hilary Biller and Lynn Melrose Densham

Reproduction Hirt & Carter (Pty) Ltd, Cape Town
Printing and binding Tien Wah Press (Pte.) Ltd, Singapore

CONTENTS

ACKNOWLEDGEMENTS

AUTHOR'S ACKNOWLEDGEMENTS

Some of my recipes have appeared in the *Angela Day* column of *The Star* newspaper. I would like to thank them for permission to use these recipes in this book. In particular, my special thanks to Lyndall Popper at *Angela Day* for her encouragement, enthusiasm and patience. It has been a pleasure working with editor, Sally Dicey. Her support, enthusiasm and professional editing have been my guiding lights through this project. Lynn Melrose Densham came in at short notice and has been a most professional and invaluable assistant in the preparation of food for photography. Thank you too to Isabel Jones for her assistance, and to Lella Leigh for testing some of the recipes. This book has been a joint venture with photographer and friend John Peacock. His artistic talent and input have made the compilation of this book a great pleasure. Diane Peacock is the hand artist whose work we used in the step-by-step photographs. To her, our mutual appreciation for the many, valuable hours of her time.

And, last but not least, I dedicate this book to my husband, Peter, for his unfailing support and patience.

I would also like to thank the following for the loan of props and appliances for photography: Mr Graham Beadle of Kenwood Home Appliances, and The Barlow Appliance Company. Grateful thanks to Peter Amoils, Karen Wales and Carolyn Wilter of The Crockery Warehouse, Lilian Blank of Villeroy and Boch, Lieberman Pottery, Pam Zimmerman Gifts, Shop Two Interiors (Craighall Park), and many special friends for the generous loan of their valuable crockery, cutlery and tableware.

PHOTOGRAPHER'S ACKNOWLEDGEMENTS

I would like to extend grateful thanks to the following people who made an enormous contribution to this book: Lynn Melrose Densham for her enthusiasm and tireless input, which, together with her invaluable experience, helped us to complete this rather large project; Milton Levanski who supplied us with the Agfa film and other photographic materials. His service and contribution (at all hours) was most appreciated; to the staff of Beith Process Laboratory for their efficient, friendly and dedicated service at all times, and for their pursuance of excellence; Teddy Ramalata for his photographic assistance during all the long hours necessary for the photographic sessions; Tim Malone for his original layout, which led to the beginning of the book; to Melissa, my daughter, who washed all those dishes; and finally to Hilary, without whom I would not even have begun. Her cheerful and dedicated approach led to a smooth and friendly working liaison at all times.

INTRODUCTION

Working on a newspaper cookery helpline gave me an insight into current food trends and what people are eating. I was amazed at the repeated requests for the old, trusted, favourite recipes and realized that a collection of these, coupled with new, interesting ideas, would make an excellent reference manual for any kitchen.

Given the creative input of photographer, John Peacock, this idea soon turned into a reality. His enthusiasm and genuine interest in food and food photography helped me greatly in consolidating the ideas into a book. We felt that a full-colour, photographic, step-by-step guide would encourage all cooks, both novices and the more experienced, to experiment with new cookery ideas.

I have included recipes suitable for both vegetarians and meat-eaters, and for every occasion, from everyday family meals to dinner party dishes. You will find classics such as vichyssoise, kedgeree and beef Wellington, as well as more modern dishes such as polenta, chicken saté sticks and Thai-style fish. I have also covered many cooking techniques, including working with yeast and gelatine, making sauces, and preparing fish and seafood.

I hope this recipe book will inspire you to indulge your creative cookery impulses, and become a trusted journal in your kitchen.

Happy cooking!

Hilary Biller

TOMATO AND SWEETCORN SOUP

This most colourful starter gets everybody talking!

SWEETCORN SOUP
2 x 410 g cans cream-style sweetcorn
250 ml (8 fl oz) single cream
500 ml (17 fl oz) full cream milk
1 tsp ground nutmeg
salt and freshly ground black pepper

TOMATO SOUP
1 large onion, finely chopped
2 tbsp butter
2 tbsp oil
2 x 410 g cans peeled tomatoes, sliced and juice reserved
600 ml (1 pint) chicken or vegetable stock, or water
1 tsp dried oregano, or 1 tbsp chopped fresh oregano
½ tsp ground cumin
2 tsp sugar
salt and freshly ground black pepper
chopped fresh chives

1 To make the sweetcorn soup, combine sweetcorn, cream, milk, nutmeg and salt and black pepper in a saucepan. Simmer for 10 minutes, allowing to heat through but not to boil. Stir occasionally. Check seasoning.

2 Prepare the tomato soup in a separate saucepan. Fry onion in butter and oil. Add tomatoes and juice, stock or water, oregano, cumin, sugar and seasoning. Simmer for 15 minutes.

3 Cool tomato soup slightly, and process in food processor. Allow to remain slightly coarse. If too thick, add more stock or water.

4 Heat individual soup bowls. Take a cup in each hand, and dip into the two soups, half filling each cup. Pour simultaneously into the heated soup bowls, allowing them to meet in the middle.

5 Garnish with chopped chives and serve immediately, with a crisp bread like Melba toast or a chunky cheese bread.

SERVES 4.

TIPS

◆ Substitute 1 kg (2¼ lb) fresh tomatoes with a good, red colour, for the canned variety. To skin, plunge first into boiling water for 2 minutes, then into cold water, and peel. If the skin doesn't peel easily, simply repeat the procedure.

◆ Melba toast is easy to make. Simply toast slices of white bread, then remove the crusts and slice the toast in half horizontally, to make two very thin slices. Place, toasted side down, on a baking sheet and bake at 160 °C (325 °F/gas 3) for about 30 minutes, until golden brown. Melba toast can also be made using a very thinly sliced French loaf – place slices on a baking sheet and bake as above until golden brown.

◆ Melba toast keeps very well if stored in an airtight container.

VICHYSSOISE

This tasty potato and leek soup is traditionally served chilled, but is also deliciously warming served piping hot on a cold winter's day.

CHICKEN STOCK
1 chicken
1 carrot, sliced
1 onion, studded with 4 cloves
1 stick celery, sliced
1 bay leaf
water

SOUP
6 leeks
2 tbsp butter
2 tbsp oil
6 potatoes, peeled and diced
salt and freshly ground black pepper
½ tsp ground nutmeg
250 ml (8 fl oz) single cream
extra cream to garnish
chopped fresh chives or paprika

1 To make chicken stock, place chicken in a large stock pot, and add vegetables and bay leaf. Cover with water, and bring to a gentle boil. Boil for 1 hour.

2 Cool slightly, then remove chicken from pot and remove all skin and meat from bones. Return bones to the pot and boil for a further 30 minutes. Skim fat off surface, then strain. You will need 1 litre (1¾ pints) stock.

3 To make soup, slice leeks, including some of the green part to give the soup a good colour, and sauté in melted butter and oil. Add the potatoes and sauté for a few minutes.

4 Pour in the stock, and add the seasoning and nutmeg. Cook for 30 minutes, or until the potatoes are tender. Cool slightly, and then process in a food processor or blender.

5 Return soup to the saucepan, add cream and heat through, taking care not to boil. Serve either well chilled or hot according to preference, garnished with cream and chopped chives or paprika.
SERVES 6.

TIPS

◆ Use freshly ground nutmeg as spices that are stored for some time can lose their flavour.

◆ Instead of garnishing with cream and chives, swirl a dollop of pesto through each serving for a delicious and tasty variation.

ROASTED BUTTERNUT SQUASH SOUP

This version of a fashionable favourite uses roasted butternut squash, giving a sublime flavour and making the soup extra special.

100 g (4 oz) butter, melted
3 tbsp golden syrup
½ tsp ground allspice
½ tsp ground cinnamon
½ tsp ground cardamom
pinch of ground nutmeg
salt and freshly ground black pepper
2 large butternut squash, halved and seeded
4 tbsp butter
1 small onion, chopped
4 sticks soup celery, sliced
2 carrots, peeled and diced
2 leeks, white part only, sliced
1.5 litres (2½ pints) chicken stock
finely grated rind and juice of 1 orange
100 ml (3½ fl oz) single cream
chopped fresh herbs or grated orange rind to garnish

1 Combine 100 g (4 oz) butter, syrup, allspice, cinnamon, cardamom, nutmeg and seasoning in a small bowl to make a glaze.

2 Place halved squash, cut side down, on a lightly greased baking sheet and roast at 200 °C (400 °F/gas 6) for 20–25 minutes.

3 Turn the butternut squash over and brush with glaze. Reduce the oven temperature to 180 °C (350 °F/gas 4). Continue roasting, brushing frequently with the glaze, until squash is tender and golden brown. Remove from the oven, and leave until cool enough to handle. Scoop out flesh with a large spoon, and set aside.

4 In a large saucepan, melt 4 tbsp butter and sauté onion for 2–3 minutes. Add the celery, carrots, leeks and squash. Sauté for 2 minutes, then place the lid on the pan and allow the vegetables to sweat for 3 minutes.

5 Add chicken stock, orange rind and juice. Simmer uncovered for approximately 35 minutes, until vegetables are soft. Purée in a food processor or blender. Check seasoning.

6 Pour into heated soup bowls. Garnish with a swirl of cream and top with some chopped fresh herbs or orange rind.
SERVES 4–6.

TIPS

- 1–2 tsp curry powder may be added with the onion in step 4 for an interesting variation.
- Butternut squash, which is a member of the gourd family, gets its name from its smooth, butter-yellow skin.
- Use a butternut squash with a deep yellow colour as it will be fully ripened and the flavour of the soup will be better.
- Pumpkin can replace the butternut squash.
- Use homemade chicken stock (see p 10) if you have it to add a delicious flavour to this soup.

WHOLESOME LENTIL SOUP

Lentils, a valuable source of protein, are classified as pulses. Red, brown and green lentils are all available, and require no pre-soaking, although red lentils do cook faster than the others. They are all suitable for this soup, so choose the ones you like best. Always pick over lentils before cooking, as they can often contain small stones.

3 tbsp oil
2 onions, chopped
2 cloves garlic, crushed
8 sticks soup celery, finely sliced
2 large carrots, grated
200 g (7 oz) lentils
2 litres ($3^1/_2$ pints) beef or chicken stock
1 bouquet garni (1 bay leaf, 2 sprigs parsley, 1 sprig rosemary and 1 sprig thyme)
1 tsp ground cumin
1 tbsp balsamic vinegar*
salt and freshly ground black pepper

1 Pre-heat the oil in a large stock pot. Add the onions and sauté until soft. Add the crushed garlic, and sauté for 1 minute. Take care not to burn the garlic, as it will become bitter.

2 Add the celery and carrots and sauté for 3 minutes. Place a lid on the pot and allow the vegetables to sweat for a further 3 minutes, to bring out the good flavour of the vegetables.

3 Add the lentils and stir-fry for 2 minutes. Pour in stock, and add bouquet garni and cumin. Simmer until lentils are tender – approximately 1–2 hours.

4 Remove the bouquet garni, stir in the balsamic vinegar, and season if necessary. Serve piping hot with bread sticks.
SERVES 3–4.

TIPS

* Balsamic vinegar is Italian red wine vinegar that is aged in barrels for 3–12 years. If it is unavailable, use cider vinegar or dark sherry.

◆ A spicy sausage, e.g. chorizo or Russian sausage, may be sliced and fried with the onion to make a spicier soup.

TRI-COLOUR MOUSSE

This cool, colourful mousse makes a perfect lunch on a hot summer's day.

TOMATO LAYER
1 tbsp gelatine
3 tbsp water
1 x 400 g can sliced tomatoes with herbs
4 spring onions, finely chopped
2 tsp finely chopped fresh basil
2 tsp finely chopped fresh oregano
1 tsp caster sugar
salt and freshly ground black pepper
1 tsp Worcestershire sauce

CUCUMBER LAYER
1 tbsp gelatine
3 tbsp water
1 large cucumber, unpeeled and grated
salt
250 ml (8 fl oz) thick natural yoghurt
250 g (9 oz) cream cheese
2–3 cloves garlic, crushed
1 tsp ground white pepper

CARROT LAYER
1 tbsp gelatine
3 tbsp water
350 g (12 oz) carrots, thinly sliced
200 ml (7 fl oz) orange juice
pinch of grated nutmeg
120 ml (4 fl oz) chicken stock
250 ml (8 fl oz) cream
chopped parsley, sliced cucumber and cocktail tomatoes to garnish

1 To make the tomato layer, sprinkle gelatine over water and leave to sponge. In a blender or food processor, blend remaining ingredients until smooth.

2 Soften gelatine sponge in a microwave on Medium for 1–2 minutes, or place it over a saucepan of hot water until soft. Add to tomato mixture and blend. Spray a large loaf tin with non-stick cooking spray. Pour in tomato mixture, cover, and leave to set in the refrigerator.

3 To make the cucumber layer, sponge gelatine in water as for the tomato layer. Place the grated cucumber in a colander, sprinkle with salt and stand for 30 minutes. Rinse under running water, drain and, using a clean cloth, squeeze out all moisture.

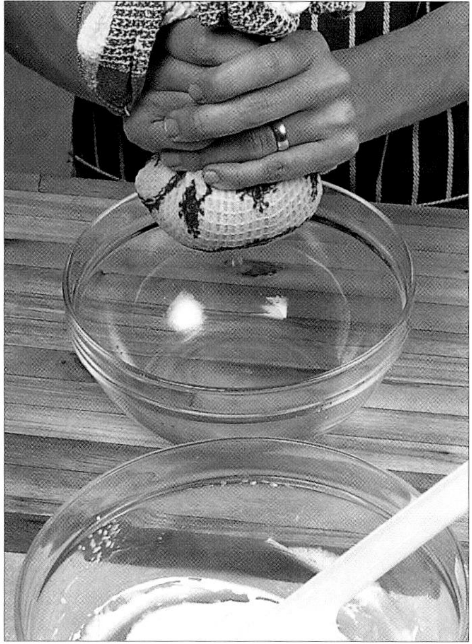

4 Combine the cucumber with remaining ingredients. Soften gelatine sponge as for the tomato layer, and fold it into the cucumber mixture. Pour the cucumber mixture over the set tomato layer, cover and refrigerate.

5 To make carrot layer, sponge gelatine in water. Combine carrots, orange juice and nutmeg in a saucepan and bring to the boil. Simmer for 20 minutes. Remove carrots with a slotted spoon, discarding juice. Place carrots with chicken stock in a blender or food processor, and blend until smooth. Soften the gelatine sponge, and add to carrot mixture with the cream. Process until just mixed. Pour the carrot mixture over set cucumber layer.

6 Cover the mousse well with cling film and refrigerate overnight. Unmould onto a serving platter, garnish with chopped parsley, if desired, thinly sliced cucumber and cocktail tomatoes, and serve in slices. SERVES 8.

CHICKEN LIVERS PERI-PERI

Eat hot and spicy Chicken Livers Peri-Peri with chunks of crusty, fresh bread to soak up all the delicious juices.

500 g (18 oz) chicken livers

MARINADE
3 tbsp wine vinegar
3 tbsp olive oil
juice of 1 lemon
2 cloves garlic, crushed
2 small, dried red chillies, seeded and finely chopped*
1 tsp ground cumin
1/2 tsp salt
freshly ground black pepper
1 tsp ground coriander
1 bay leaf

SAUCE
1 onion, finely chopped
4 tsp olive oil
4 tsp butter
1 tbsp tomato paste
2 tsp Worcestershire sauce
dash of Tabasco sauce
120 ml (4 fl oz) chicken stock
1 tbsp brandy
fresh coriander, onion rings and a small red chilli to garnish

1 Wash the chicken livers, and remove membranes and all discoloured and dark bits.

2 To make the marinade, combine all ingredients, and marinate the chicken livers for 2 hours. Drain livers and set aside, reserving the marinade.

3 To make the sauce, sauté onion in oil and butter until soft but not brown. Add livers and cook over high heat for 2 minutes.

4 Reduce the heat, and add the tomato paste, Worcestershire sauce, Tabasco, reserved marinade and chicken stock.

5 Simmer for 5 minutes. Pour in the brandy, heat through, and then spoon into individual, heated serving bowls, and serve garnished with coriander, onion rings and chilli. Crusty rolls or thick slices of fresh, homemade bread are an essential accompaniment to mop up the spicy juices.
SERVES 4 AS A STARTER.

TIPS

* The amount of chilli can be altered to taste, and chilli powder can be used if preferred. Take care as it can be powerful!

◆ An interesting serving suggestion is to thread 3–4 marinated chicken livers onto small skewers (if using wooden skewers, first soak them in cold water for 30 minutes to prevent them from burning), then arrange the chicken skewers in an ovenproof dish, pour the marinade over, and grill for about 2 minutes either side, basting frequently. Serve with any extra marinade spooned over the top.

AVOCADO RITZ

This dish, using the delicious fruit of the sub-tropical avocado tree, makes an excellent starter, or stands alone as a light luncheon meal.

3 ripe avocados
lemon juice

SAUCE
2 extra-large egg yolks
1 tsp mustard powder
1 tsp salt
pinch of white pepper
1 tbsp lemon juice
5 tsp tomato sauce
100 ml (3½ fl oz) single cream
120 ml (4 fl oz) oil
paprika

FILLING
150 g (5 oz) shrimps, cooked
150 g (5 oz) hake or monkfish, cubed and poached

GARNISH
shredded lettuce
6 large prawns, cooked with shell on, deveined and head removed
stuffed olive slices
1 tbsp Danish lumpfish roe

1 Halve the avocados, remove the stones and hollow out the centres slightly to accommodate the filling. Brush with lemon juice to prevent discoloration.

2 To make sauce, beat egg yolks lightly with mustard powder, salt and white pepper. Place in the top of a double boiler over barely boiling water. Add lemon juice, tomato sauce and cream. Add oil in a steady stream, stirring constantly until the sauce thickens. Stir in paprika. Cool.

3 To make the filling, combine the shrimps and fish with the cooled sauce. Pile the filling into the avocado halves and arrange on a serving dish.

4 Garnish with shredded lettuce. Place a large prawn decoratively on top of each half, then top with olive slice and lumpfish roe. Serve immediately.
SERVES 6.

TIPS

◆ Canned tuna or salmon can replace the shrimps, and also makes a good filling: flake and add to the sauce in step 3.

◆ Replace the fish with 300 g (11 oz) commercially available seafood mix containing, for example, mussels, shrimps and calamari.

◆ A good quality mayonnaise can replace the sauce: combine 250 ml (8 fl oz) mayonnaise with 1 tsp tomato sauce, 2 tbsp single cream, ½ tsp Tabasco sauce, ½ tsp prepared mustard and salt and pepper.

◆ To test an avocado for ripeness, squeeze very gently. If it is slightly soft, it is ripe.

◆ There are numerous varieties of avocados, and the appearance and texture of the skin can range from a thick, smooth, glossy green to a wrinkled black or purple. Choose those with unblemished skins.

◆ Avocados are most often eaten raw, but can also be cooked. They are delicious baked with a creamy filling topped with cheese or fresh breadcrumbs at 180 °C (350 °F/gas 4) for 10–15 minutes.

◆ If you heat a lemon gently in very hot water before squeezing, it will yield more juice.

ROULADE

This is made with a soufflé mixture, which is baked, then spread with a savoury filling and rolled up like a Swiss roll. A plain roulade can be filled with almost any filling and makes an excellent starter.

75 g (3 oz) butter
75 g (3 oz) flour
450 ml (15 fl oz) milk
4 extra-large eggs
salt and pepper

FILLING
125 g (4½ oz) cream cheese or crème fraîche*
4 tbsp sour cream
1 tbsp fresh lemon juice
100 g (4 oz) can tuna, pink salmon or sardines, drained and flaked
1 tbsp chopped fresh dill
1 tbsp chopped fresh parsley
salt and freshly ground black pepper

1 Melt the butter in a saucepan. Add the flour and stir to form a roux. Add all the milk at once, whisking constantly with a wire whisk until the white sauce thickens, then remove from the heat and cool slightly.

2 Separate the eggs, lightly beat the egg yolks, then add to the white sauce. Stiffly beat the egg whites, then fold into the white sauce, and season.

3 Line a 23 x 32 cm (9 x 13 in) Swiss roll tin with greaseproof paper or an ovenproof baking bag, and oil lightly with a pastry brush. Pour the mixture into the tin and bake at 160 °C (325 °F/gas 3) for 40–45 minutes, until golden brown.

4 Combine the cream cheese, or crème fraîche if using, sour cream, lemon juice, fish, dill, parsley and seasoning. Mix well.

5 Turn the cooked soufflé out onto a piece of greaseproof paper. Trim off the hard edges – approximately 1–2 cm (½–¾ in) all around. Spread evenly with the filling. Roll up, starting at one of the longer ends. Serve whole or sliced as a starter.
MAKES 10–12 SLICES.

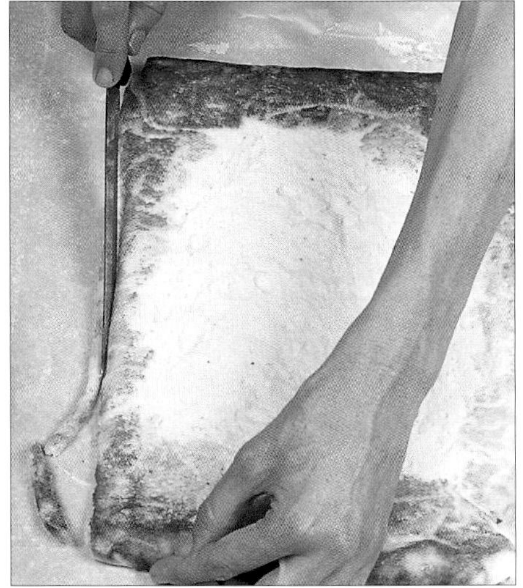

TIPS

* Use either commercially available crème fraîche, or make your own by combining 120 ml (4 fl oz) double cream with 1 tbsp buttermilk in a glass jar. Cover with a lid and stand for 1–2 days in a warm place.

◆ To make a spinach roulade, cook 400 g (14 oz) fresh spinach, then drain well and liquidize. Fold spinach into the white sauce, then proceed with step 2. To make filling, replace the fish with 250 g (9 oz) cooked mushrooms and proceed.
◆ Almost any fish can be used in the filling – try slithers of smoked salmon or trout, or poached haddock, whichever you prefer.

◆ The roulade freezes very well.

POLENTA WITH TOMATO SAUCE

Yellow Italian polenta meal is available from delicatessens and speciality stores, although it may be replaced by coarse yellow maize meal.

500 ml (17 fl oz) water
500 ml (17 fl oz) milk
2 tsp salt
250 g (9 oz) polenta or maize meal
4 tbsp butter
50 g (2 oz) grated Parmesan cheese
½ beaten egg
½ tsp ground nutmeg
salt and freshly ground black pepper
extra butter

SAUCE
1 onion, finely chopped
3 tbsp oil
2 cloves garlic, crushed
1 x 400 g can whole, peeled Italian tomatoes, sliced and juice reserved
1 tsp sugar
dash of Worcestershire sauce
1 tsp dried oregano, or 1 tbsp chopped fresh oregano
salt and freshly ground black pepper
250 ml (8 fl oz) red or white wine, chicken stock, or water
extra Parmesan cheese and a sprig of basil to garnish

1 To make polenta, bring water, milk and salt to the boil in a saucepan with a lid. Sprinkle in the polenta or maize meal while stirring constantly with a wooden spoon to prevent lumps. Reduce heat, cover, and simmer for about 25 minutes, stirring occasionally.

2 Remove the polenta from the heat, and stir in the butter, Parmesan cheese, egg, nutmeg and salt and pepper.

3 Pour polenta into a greased 23 x 32 cm (9 x 13 in) baking sheet, spreading out as evenly as possible. Cover, and cool. Cut cooled polenta into squares.

4 Place the extra butter in an ovenproof dish. Pre-heat the dish in an oven at 180 °C (350 °F/gas 4) until the butter is melted. Add the polenta squares and re-heat for 10–15 minutes.

5 Meanwhile, make the tomato sauce: sauté the onion in pre-heated oil, then add the garlic and tomatoes with juice. Add the sugar, Worcestershire sauce, oregano, salt and pepper, wine, or chicken stock or water if using, and simmer until the sauce is thickened.

6 To serve, place a spoonful of tomato sauce in the base of individual serving dishes. Place 4–6 hot polenta blocks on top of the sauce. Top with more tomato sauce. Sprinkle generously with grated or shaved Parmesan, top with basil, and serve immediately.
SERVES 4 AS A STARTER.

TIPS

- As polenta is a filling dish, serve as a starter before a light main course.
- Polenta may be served with a variety of sauces of your choice, and is also delicious served piping hot with melted butter, herbs and cheese.

OMELETTES

One of the quickest meals to delight any palate. Choose between a flat or a fluffy omelette, and fill it with a delicious, savoury filling.

FLAT OMELETTE
2 extra-large eggs
2 tbsp water
salt and pepper
1 tbsp butter

FLUFFY OMELETTE
3 extra-large eggs, separated
salt and pepper
1 tbsp butter

FILLINGS
grated cheese, chopped fried bacon, chopped ham, chopped tomatoes, chopped fresh herbs of your choice, cooked sliced mushrooms, flaked cooked fish, chopped cooked chicken livers, cooked sliced potatoes, sliced asparagus, creamed spinach, chopped spring onions

FLAT OMELETTE

1 Lightly whisk the eggs with a fork until just combined. Add the water and salt and pepper, and whisk again.

2 Pre-heat butter in a 20 cm (8 in), non-stick frying pan placed on top of the stove. Pour in the egg mixture.

3 As the omelette begins to cook, loosen the edges with a plastic spatula so that the uncooked egg mixture runs to the bottom of the pan. Cook for 1–1½ minutes, until done to your taste.

4 If adding a filling, spread it on half of the omelette, then fold the other half over the filling with the spatula. Carefully slide the omelette onto a heated plate and serve immediately.
MAKES 1 OMELETTE.

FLUFFY OMELETTE

1 Whip egg yolks lightly with salt and pepper.

2 Whip the egg whites with an electric mixer until soft peaks form. Gently fold the egg whites into the egg yolk mixture.

3 Pre-heat the butter in a 20 cm (8 in), non-stick frying pan on the top of the stove. At the same time, pre-heat the grill. Pour the egg mixture into the pan and cook for 1–2 minutes on the hob, until the bottom of the omelette is golden brown. Then place the omelette under the pre-heated grill and brown lightly.

4 If you are filling the omelette, spread the prepared filling on half of the omelette, then gently fold the other half over with a spatula. Carefully slide the filled omelette onto a heated plate and serve immediately.
MAKES 1 OMELETTE.

TIPS

- Make sure that the recipient of the omelette is sitting at the table ready and waiting – omelettes must be eaten immediately as they spoil very quickly and so cannot be left.
- Fresh eggs are heavy and become lighter as they get older. To test for freshness, place an egg in lightly salted cold water. If it sinks, it is fresh; if it floats on the top, it is bad.

EGGS BENEDICT

A favourite for weekend breakfasts when time is on your side.

4 slices of ham, or
  4 slices of short back bacon
2 English muffins, or
  4 thin slices of white bread
butter for frying and spreading
4 extra-large eggs
1 tbsp white vinegar
4 sprigs of parsley to garnish

HOLLANDAISE SAUCE
125 g (4½ oz) butter
3 tbsp water
2 extra-large egg yolks
salt and white pepper
1 tbsp lemon juice

1 Cut the ham or bacon to fit the muffins, then fry the meat in a little butter. Split the muffins and toast them on one side only, or toast the bread on both sides and remove the crusts.

2 To poach the eggs, bring approximately 7.5 cm (3 in) water to a slow boil in a frying pan, then add the vinegar.

3 Break the eggs into the bubbling water. All four eggs can be poached together. Reduce the heat to a gentle simmer and poach for 4 minutes – the white should be set and the yolk soft. Transfer poached eggs to a bowl of hot water to keep warm.

4 To make the Hollandaise sauce, melt the butter in a heavy-based saucepan. Set aside.

5 In a separate, small saucepan, whisk together the water, egg yolks and seasoning. Place over low heat and cook for 3 minutes, stirring constantly.

6 Remove from the heat, add cooled butter in a stream, and whisk. Stir in lemon juice.

7 To assemble, top each muffin half or slice of toast with ham or bacon, then with a hot poached egg and lastly with Hollandaise sauce. Garnish with a sprig of parsley, or any other fresh herb of your choice, and serve at once on heated plates.

SERVES 2–4, DEPENDING ON APPETITES.

TIP

- Replace ham or bacon with spinach leaves which have been washed, cooked, well drained and dried. Top the spinach with a piece of poached, smoked haddock, then with a poached egg, for a more substantial meal.

EGG MOUSSE WITH CAVIAR TOPPING

This is an excellent addition to a brunch or cocktail party menu. True caviar, most often the roe of the Beluga sturgeon, is extremely expensive, but it can be replaced by Danish lumpfish roe, which is dyed black or red, and is readily available at a more affordable price.

- 6 hard-boiled eggs, chopped
- 1 small onion, finely chopped
- 1 bunch of chives, finely chopped
- 4 tbsp thick, good quality mayonnaise
- 2 tsp Worcestershire sauce
- dash of Tabasco sauce
- salt and freshly ground black pepper
- 120 ml (4 fl oz) whipping cream
- 1 x 100 g (4 oz) jar red Danish lumpfish roe
- 1 x 100 g (4 oz) jar black Danish lumpfish roe

1 To make the mousse, combine the eggs with onion, chives, mayonnaise, Worcestershire sauce and Tabasco. Season. The mixture should be stiff enough to hold its shape. Place on a serving dish and pat into a thick, circular layer.

2 Whip the cream until stiff, then spread over the egg mousse. Cover loosely, and chill for at least 1 hour.

3 To garnish the mousse, cut out a cardboard circle with the same circumference as the mousse. Cut a quadrant out of the cardboard circle. Hold the cardboard circle over the mousse and spoon red roe into the gap left by the quadrant.

4 Lift and rotate the cardboard to uncover the next section of the mousse, then spoon black roe into the gap. Continue until the egg mousse is covered with 4 alternating quadrants of roe. Serve with Melba toast.

SERVES 8–10 AS A SNACK WITH DRINKS.

TIPS

- The egg mousse can be prepared to the end of step 1 up to 24 hours in advance. Cover well and refrigerate.
- Instead of topping the egg mousse with cream and caviar, spoon the mousse onto a pedastal serving dish, top with a layer of cooked pink shrimps tossed in seafood mayonnaise, and garnish with a layer of chopped fresh parsley or dill.
- Store onions in a separate place, as they have a pungent flavour that is easily absorbed by other foods.
- Rub your hands with lemon juice or vinegar after chopping onions, to remove the smell.

BAKED MOZZARELLA CHEESE

Serve Baked Mozzarella Cheese with bread, to spread the cheese and to soak up the flavoured oil.

500 g (18 oz) mozzarella cheese*
100 ml ($3^1/_2$ fl oz) olive oil
6 cloves garlic, crushed
2 tbsp chilli sauce** (optional)
1 tbsp chopped fresh oregano
1 tbsp chopped fresh thyme
1 tbsp chopped fresh rosemary
1 bay leaf

1 Pierce mozzarella cheese all over with a meat skewer, to allow the seasoned olive oil to penetrate the cheese.

2 Combine the olive oil, garlic, chilli sauce, herbs and bay leaf in an ovenproof baking dish just big enough to accommodate the mozzarella cheese.

3 Marinate the cheese in the seasoned olive oil for at least 6–12 hours, or overnight, turning frequently to allow the marinade to penetrate the whole cheese.

4 Just before serving, pre-heat the oven to 160 °C (325 °F/gas 3). Remove bay leaf, then bake the cheese in the marinade for 15–20 minutes, until completely soft and melted. Serve immediately with bread.

5 If the cheese hardens before it has been eaten, re-heat it in the oven at 160 °C (325 °F/gas 3). Take care not to over-heat as it can become very hard.
SERVES 6 AS A STARTER.

TIPS

* Try another cheese for a change – Ricotta or a soft feta.

** Use a moderate chilli sauce so as not to steal all the flavour from the cheese.

◆ Mozzarella cheese has an elastic texture, a delicate flavour, and a pale, almost milky, colour. It melts readily when cooked, making it perfect for pizzas as well as for baking. Fresh mozzarella must be eaten within a day or two, but processed mozzarella can be refrigerated for up to 2 weeks.

◆ Garlic is a principal ingredient of this aromatic dish, not merely a flavouring, so don't omit or reduce it.

SAVOURY FILO PARCELS

2 tbsp olive oil
6 spring onions, finely chopped
1 clove garlic, crushed
1 small carrot, finely grated
4 red tomatoes, peeled and chopped
1 tsp sugar
1 tsp dried oregano, or 1 tbsp chopped fresh oregano
200 g (7 oz) strong-flavoured cheese, e.g. fontina or Cheddar, grated
3 tbsp bean sprouts
salt and freshly ground black pepper
4 sheets filo pastry
100 g (4 oz) butter, melted

FRESH TOMATO COULIS
500 g (18 oz) red tomatoes, peeled, seeded and chopped
salt and white pepper
2 tbsp finely chopped parsley or basil
1 tsp caster sugar
1 tsp Worcestershire sauce
1 fresh green chilli, seeded and chopped

1 To prepare filling, heat oil, sauté spring onions until soft, and then add garlic. Add carrot and sauté for 2 minutes.

2 Add chopped tomatoes, sugar and oregano, and simmer for 5 minutes. Remove from the heat and, while still hot, stir in cheese. Allow to cool.

3 Fold in bean sprouts and salt and black pepper.

4 Cut each sheet of filo pastry into 4 squares, and allow 2 squares for each parcel. Brush the pastry with melted butter, and place the first square of pastry on top of the second.

5 To assemble parcels, place a large spoonful of filling into the centre of a prepared square. Gather up the corners, twist lightly to make a parcel, then brush with more melted butter. Place on a lightly greased baking sheet, and bake at 190 °C (375 °F/gas 5) for 10–15 minutes. Cover with foil caps if browning too quickly.

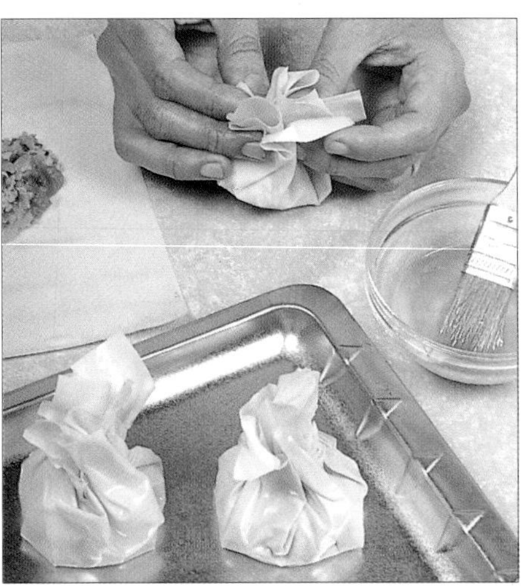

6 To make the coulis, season the tomatoes with salt and pepper. Stand in a colander for 30 minutes to drain excess moisture. Add the herbs, sugar, Worcestershire sauce and chilli. Process in a food processor or blender. Pour into a saucepan and heat until piping hot.

7 To serve, pour a little hot coulis onto an individual serving plate. Place the hot filo parcel on top of the coulis and serve immediately.
MAKES 8 PARCELS.

TIPS

- Filo pastry is a thin, delicate pastry made with flour, water and salt. It contains no fat and therefore the layers must be brushed with melted butter or sunflower oil.
- Filo pastry dries out very quickly, so keep it covered with with a clean, damp kitchen towel while you are working.
- Wrap filo well in cling film and freeze for up to 1 year.

AVOCADO AND BLUE CHEESE MOUSSE

The complementary flavours of blue cheese and avocado are perfectly balanced in this attractive, layered starter, which is also well suited to a buffet display.

AVOCADO LAYER

3 avocados, peeled and stoned
3 tbsp lemon juice
2 tbsp finely chopped parsley
250 ml (8 fl oz) buttermilk
120 ml (4 fl oz) homemade or good quality mayonnaise
½ tsp cayenne pepper
salt
2 tsp Worcestershire sauce
4 tsp gelatine
4 tbsp water

BLUE CHEESE LAYER

125 g (4½ oz) creamy blue cheese, crumbled
250 ml (8 fl oz) thick plain yoghurt
2 cloves garlic, crushed
3 sticks celery, trimmed and finely chopped
2 tbsp chopped fresh chives
salt and freshly ground black pepper
1 tbsp gelatine
4 tbsp water
250 ml (8 fl oz) whipping cream
watercress to garnish

1 To make the avocado layer, process the avocados in the food processor until smooth. Add the remaining ingredients, except the gelatine and water, and continue to process until smooth.

2 Sprinkle the gelatine over the water and stand until it forms a sponge. Soften the gelatine sponge either in a microwave on Medium for 1 minute, or by standing it over a pan of hot water off the cooker. Fold the softened gelatine into the avocado mixture.

3 Spray a 2 litre (3½ pint) ring mould with non-stick cooking spray. Pour the avocado mixture into the mould, cover, and refrigerate until firm.

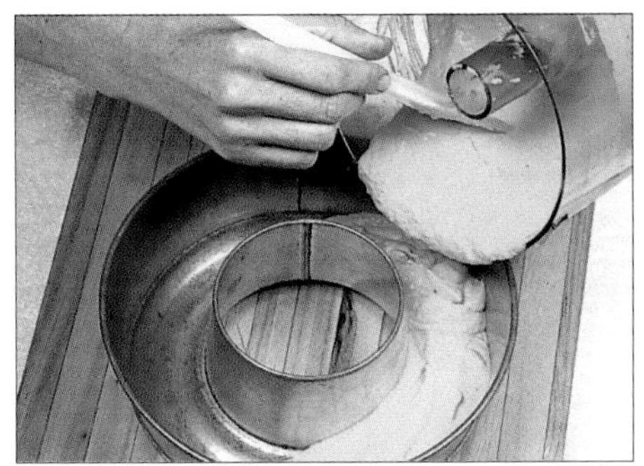

4 To make the blue cheese layer, pulse blue cheese and yoghurt in the processor until combined. Add garlic, celery, chives and seasoning, and combine well.

5 Sprinkle the gelatine over the water and leave until it forms a sponge. Soften the gelatine sponge either in a microwave on Medium for 1 minute, or by standing it over a pan of hot water off the cooker.

6 Keeping the food processor running, pour the softened gelatine through the feed tube in a thin stream into the blue cheese mixture. Whip the cream until it is slightly thickened, then fold it gently into the processed blue cheese mixture.

7 Pour the blue cheese mixture over the set avocado layer. Cover and refrigerate overnight, or until the mixture is set.

8 Turn out onto a large serving platter. Garnish with the watercress. Serve with savoury biscuits, crispy Melba toast or coarse brown bread.

SERVES 8 AS A STARTER, OR 10–12 AS A SNACK WITH DRINKS.

TIPS

- If you do not like blue cheese, replace it with any other soft cheese, but check the seasoning as more may be required.
- Eat the mousse within 24 hours of making, or the avocado will start to discolour.

CRUSTLESS SAVOURY TART

This simple dish always draws compliments. I can make it in my sleep, and its simplicity and flavour make it a winner. It is an ideal savoury snack for tea parties.

- 1 large onion, finely chopped
- 2 tbsp oil
- 1 clove garlic, crushed
- 1 green or red pepper, seeded and finely chopped
- 250 g (9 oz) button mushrooms, sliced
- 125 g (4½ oz) ham, cubed, or smoked Vienna sausages, sliced
- 100 g (4 oz) mature Cheddar cheese, grated
- 3 extra-large eggs
- 2 tbsp plain flour
- 1 tsp mustard powder
- 500 ml (17 fl oz) milk
- 1 tsp mixed dried herbs
- 2 tbsp chopped fresh parsley
- salt and freshly ground black pepper
- ½ tsp paprika

1 Fry the onion in pre-heated oil until soft and golden. Add the garlic and pepper and fry for 2 minutes. Add mushrooms and fry until the liquid has evaporated.

2 Add the cubed ham or sausage slices, and fry for a further 2–3 minutes.

3 Using a slotted spoon, spoon the mixture into a greased 2 litre (3½ pint) ovenproof dish. Sprinkle the cheese over the top.

4 In a mixing bowl combine the eggs, flour and mustard powder. Mix with a balloon whisk until the mixture is smooth.

5 Add the milk, herbs, parsley, seasoning and paprika. Whisk until they are well mixed. Pour over the onion and cheese mixture in the ovenproof dish.

6 Bake at 180 °C (350 °F/gas 4) for 45 minutes, until puffed and golden brown. Slice, and serve warm as a snack.

SERVES 6–8.

TIPS

◆ The ham or Vienna sausages can be omitted or replaced with drained and flaked tuna fish or flaked smoked haddock.

◆ This is a very versatile pie: the onions, cheese, milk and eggs are the essential ingredients; the rest can be replaced with what is in the refrigerator or pantry.

VEGETABLE TART

This is a variation of Quiche Lorraine, the world's most popular open savoury tart. The pastry is a versatile basic shortcrust one that can be made into a sweet pastry with the simple addition of 1–2 tbsp caster sugar.

PASTRY
125 g (4½ oz) plain flour
1 tsp salt
4 tbsp butter
3 tbsp cold water
1 large egg yolk
2 tsp lemon juice

FILLING
125 g (4½ oz) button mushrooms, sliced
1 tbsp butter
4 courgettes, sliced
100 g (4 oz) broccoli, broken into florets
3 extra-large eggs
500 ml (17 fl oz) milk
1 tsp mustard powder
salt and freshly ground black pepper
½ tsp ground nutmeg

1 Sift together the flour and salt. Rub in the butter until the mixture resembles breadcrumbs. Mix the water, yolk and lemon juice, and then add to the crumbed mixture, combining with a round-tipped knife. Form the pastry into a ball, and knead gently on a lightly floured surface.

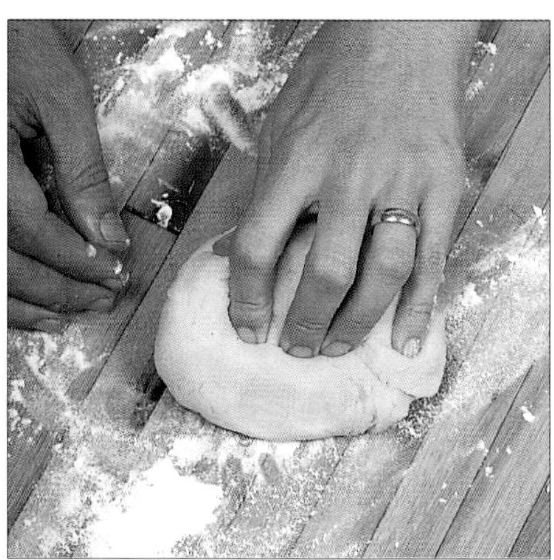

2 Roll the pastry out to fit a 23 cm (9 in) pie dish. Press in, then cover and refrigerate for 20–30 minutes.

3 To prepare the filling, fry the mushrooms in the butter until soft. Add the courgettes and broccoli, and stir-fry for 2 minutes. Remove the vegetables with a slotted spoon, place in the chilled pastry shell, and set aside.

4 Combine the eggs, milk, mustard powder, seasoning and nutmeg in a bowl. Whisk with a balloon whisk until smooth. Pour over the vegetables.

5 Place the tart on a baking sheet, and bake at 180 °C (350 °F/gas 4) for 45 minutes. Serve warm with a mixed salad for a light meal, or sliced as a savoury snack with tea or coffee.
SERVES 4 AS A LIGHT MEAL, OR 6–8 AS A SAVOURY SNACK.

TIPS

◆ The tart freezes well: cover and freeze for 3–6 months.

◆ For a more colourful vegetable tart, replace the courgettes with 1 finely chopped red pepper and 6 medium, yellow patty pan squash, and proceed as above.

◆ To make a Quiche Lorraine, fry 1 finely chopped, small onion in 1 tbsp oil, then add 125 g (4½ oz) chopped streaky bacon or ham. Fry the bacon, if using, until crispy, or the ham until heated, then remove and cool. Place the bacon or ham and the onion in the pastry case. Proceed as above with step 4.

◆ To clean mushrooms, wipe with a damp cloth. If they are very sandy, plunge into cold water before wiping. They are very absorbent, so don't soak.

FISH CAKES WITH TARTARE SAUCE

A great way to use up leftover fish, or to make a delicious and more interesting meal of hake.

500 g (18 oz) hake
250 g (9 oz) smoked haddock
1 bay leaf
3 slices lemon
1 onion, sliced
1 carrot, sliced
5 tsp chopped fresh parsley
2 cm (3/4 in) piece of brown bread, grated
5 tsp chopped fresh chives
1 tsp paprika
dash of Tabasco sauce
mashed potatoes (using 4 medium potatoes, 3 tbsp butter and 120 ml (4 fl oz) milk)
1 extra-large egg, beaten (optional)
flour
1 extra-large egg, beaten
oil

TARTARE SAUCE
150 ml (5 fl oz) good quality mayonnaise
1 tsp finely chopped chives
1 tbsp chopped fresh parsley
1 tsp chopped capers
1 tbsp chopped gherkins
1 tbsp fresh lemon juice

1 Place the hake and haddock in a saucepan and cover with water. Add the bay leaf, lemon, onion and carrot.

2 Poach until just cooked – the fish will flake easily when prodded with a fork (approximately 15 minutes if cooked from frozen.)

3 Remove fish from the pan with a slotted spoon, cool, then flake with a fork, removing skin and bones. Place in a bowl and add parsley, breadcrumbs, chives, paprika and Tabasco.

4 Add mashed potatoes. If the mixture is too dry, add a beaten egg – it should be firm enough to form patties. Shape into patties, dip into flour and rest in the refrigerator for about 30 minutes. This helps the patties keep their shape while frying.

5 Dip the patties in the second beaten egg and dust with more flour. Shallow fry in hot oil. Drain on absorbent paper and serve hot with Tartare sauce.

6 To make Tartare sauce, place mayonnaise in a mixing bowl. Add all the remaining ingredients and combine. Place in a serving dish and stand for at least 1 hour before serving. This allows the flavours to mingle and improve.
SERVES 4.

TIP

◆ Smoked haddock adds a good flavour to fish cakes, and the ratio of hake to haddock easily can be changed. The flavour of the fish cakes improves on standing: allow a standing period of 3 hours before cooking.

FISH AND CHIPS

Fried fish served with its universal accompaniment, chips, can be a delicious family meal if cooked correctly: deep-frying white-fleshed types of fish in a tasty, protective batter is highly recommended.

575 g (1¼ lb) firm white fish fillets

BATTER
125 g (4½ oz) plain flour
½ tsp baking powder
1 tsp salt
½ tsp white pepper
1 egg
250 ml (8 fl oz) milk
1 tsp oil
oil for frying

CHIPS
4–6 large potatoes
salted iced water
oil for frying

1 Cut the fillets into serving portions, then dry on absorbent paper.

2 Prepare the batter by sifting the flour, baking powder, salt and pepper into a bowl. Combine the egg, milk and oil in a separate bowl. Make a well in the dry ingredients, pour in the egg mixture, and whisk with a balloon whisk until smooth.

3 Pre-heat oil in a deep frying pan until hot enough to brown a cube of white bread in 1 minute. Dip fish fillets into the batter, then fry in the hot oil for 3–5 minutes, turning once to brown both sides. Remove, place on absorbent paper to drain off oil, and keep warm in a slow oven or a warming drawer.

4 To make the chips, peel potatoes and cut into 5 x 1 cm (2 x ½ in) strips. Place in salted iced water for up to 30 minutes, then remove and drain well. Dry completely on a clean kitchen towel.

5 Fry the chips in pre-heated oil until just limp and glazed-looking. Remove, and place on a baking sheet covered with a piece of absorbent paper. Re-heat the oil just before serving, and fry chips until crisp and golden brown.

6 Drain chips on absorbent paper once more. Sprinkle lightly with salt.

7 Serve pieces of the battered, fried fish on heated plates, accompanied by generous portions of hot chips. Garnish with plenty of lemon and accompany it with Tartare sauce if desired (see p. 42). Serve with a mixed green salad.
SERVES 4.

TIPS

- Instead of using a batter, fish can be fried with just a coating of breadcrumbs or seasoned flour: combine flour, if using, with salt and pepper; dry fish well, dip in beaten egg and then in flour or breadcrumbs; refrigerate for 30 minutes to set the coating, then proceed with step 3 as above.

- Frozen fish fillets can be used. For a better result when using frozen fillets, do not defrost simply increase the frying time to 10 minutes.

- When making the batter, the liquid used can be varied for different results: water makes a light batter, milk makes a smooth batter, and beer adds flavour and air; a combination of water and milk can be used too.

MY GRANDMOTHER'S PICKLED FISH

My maternal grandmother was an excellent cook of traditional South African food, and I have vivid memories of delicious Sunday lunches in my grandparents' Pretoria home. Her refrigerator was always packed full with culinary treats, and this pickled fish was one of them.

60 g (2½ oz) plain flour
salt and white pepper
1.5–2 kg (3¼–4½ lb) firm white fish fillets, sliced into serving pieces
oil for frying

SAUCE
1 kg (2¼ lb) onions, sliced into thick rings
375 ml (13 fl oz) water
2 tbsp curry powder
100 g (4 oz) soft brown sugar
1 cm (½ in) piece of fresh ginger, peeled and grated
3 bay or lemon leaves
1 tsp ground coriander
6 black peppercorns
salt and freshly ground black pepper
1 chilli, finely chopped*
500 ml (17 fl oz) good quality vinegar
1 tbsp cornflour

1 Season the flour with salt and pepper. Dip the fish fillets into the seasoned flour, coating both sides. Pre-heat the oil, and fry fish on both sides until golden brown and cooked. Place on absorbent paper to cool.

2 Boil the onion rings in the water for 3 minutes.

3 Add all the remaining ingredients to the onions and water, except cornflour. Bring to the boil and simmer for 5 minutes.

4 Slake cornflour with 2 tbsp water and add to the onion and curry mixture. Simmer, uncovered, for a further 5 minutes.

5 Arrange the fish and the onion curry sauce in layers in a large dish, or in a sterilized glass jar with a lid.

6 Marinate, covered, in the refrigerator for 3 days before serving. Serve with a selection of salads and chunky slices of wholemeal bread.
SERVES 6–8.

TIPS

* For a less spicy pickled fish, omit the chilli.

◆ Avoid storing large quantities of spices – they lose their colour and flavour if kept for too long. Store in airtight containers, away from direct sunlight. It is best to buy small quantities of spices as you need them.

◆ Prepare the sauce in an earthenware or enamel pan, and not a metal one, as the high vinegar content will cause a reaction with any metal. Stir with a wooden spoon.

◆ This sauce can be adapted to make excellent pickled vegetables. Use almost any fresh vegetables – pickling onions, cucumbers, courgettes, cauliflower florets and sweet peppers are particularly good. Prepare the vegetables, then pack in layers in an earthenware or enamel dish, sprinkling salt between each layer and over the top. Leave to stand for 24 hours to draw out excess water from the vegetables. Pour off the salted water and drain well. Prepare the sauce as above, but exclude the onion rings, curry powder and cornflour. Pack the vegetables into hot, sterilized jars (if you are pickling onions, first soften by boiling in vinegar for 1–2 minutes) and then add the hot sauce. Seal and leave to stand for 2 weeks before using.

SWEET HERRINGS

Herrings are oily fish such as sardines and mackerel. Most herrings are eaten pickled or cured, rather than fresh.

6 salt herrings
200 g (7 oz) white sugar
150 ml (5 fl oz) red wine
175 ml (6 fl oz) cider vinegar
10 whole black peppercorns
1 tbsp pickling spice
1/2 tsp mustard seeds
2 large onions, sliced into rings
1 large Granny Smith apple, peeled and cut into small cubes
1 tbsp chopped fresh dill
2 bay leaves

1 Soak herrings in cold water overnight. Pour off the water.

2 Usually the head is removed before a herring is salted, but if this has not been done, cut off the head, or break it off using your thumb and forefinger. If the intestines have not been removed, cut a slit along the belly and scoop them out. Open the fish flat along the belly. Pull out the backbone, starting at the head end, and loosening it with your fingers. Snap backbone at tail. Cut each fish into two fillets. Rinse and dry.

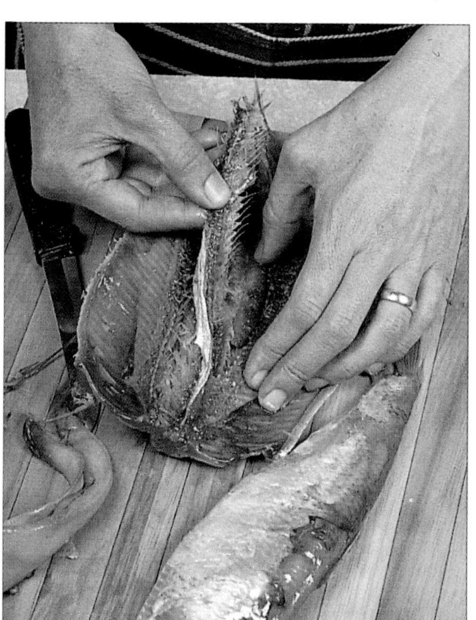

3 Cut the herring fillets into small strips about 2 cm (3/4 in) wide. Set aside.

4 Combine the white sugar, red wine and cider vinegar in a saucepan. Stir over a moderate heat until the sugar has dissolved. Add the peppercorns, pickling spice, mustard seeds, onion rings, cubed apple, chopped fresh dill and bay leaves. Simmer for 3 minutes to make a marinade.

5 Place the herring strips in a non-metallic bowl. Pour the marinade over the fish, cover, and marinate in the refrigerator for 4–5 days. Turn the herring strips every day.

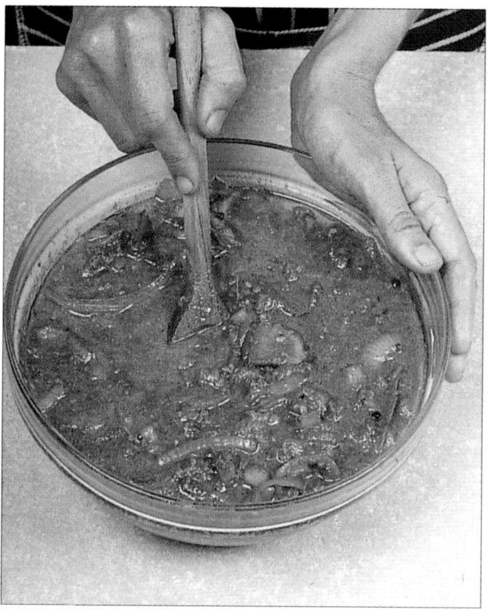

6 Serve sweet herrings as a starter, garnishing the side of the plate with a green salad (lettuce, cucumber slices, spring onion and green pepper), or as a light luncheon dish, accompanied by a beetroot or carrot salad, and fresh bread and butter.

SERVES 6–8 AS A STARTER.

TIPS

- For extra spice, add 2 seeded and chopped chillies at step 3.
- To simplify the preparation of this dish, buy 12 ready-soaked salt herring fillets, slice them into thin strips, and proceed with step 4 as above.
- Pickling spice, perfect for marinades and preserves, consists of combinations of spices which are left whole so as not to cloud the pickling liquid.

THAI-STYLE FISH

Eastern flavours have made a strong impact on Western food. This dish marries the two for a unique taste.

6 firm white fish fillets

MARINADE
grated rind and juice of 1 lemon
2 cloves garlic, crushed
85 ml (3 fl oz) clear honey
4 tbsp soy sauce
1 tbsp chopped fresh coriander
1 fresh red chilli, seeded and chopped
2 cm (3/4 in) piece of fresh ginger, peeled and grated

VEGETABLES
100 g (4 oz) cucumber, unpeeled, seeded and sliced
100 g (4 oz) French beans, topped and tailed
1 red pepper, seeded and julienned
1 bunch of spring onions, trimmed
100 g (4 oz) baby carrots, scrubbed
100 g (4 oz) baby sweetcorn

1 Place the fillets in a dish large enough to accommodate the fish without overlapping.

2 Combine lemon rind and juice, garlic, honey, soy sauce, coriander, chilli and ginger in a bowl. Pour over fish, and marinate for 1–2 hours, turning twice.

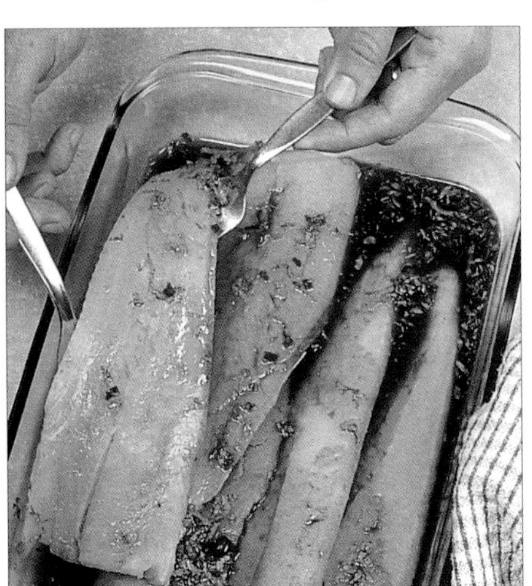

3 Remove fillets from the dish, reserving the marinade. Grill the fillets under high heat for 3–4 minutes per side. Place cooked fish on a heated serving dish in the warming drawer, and prepare vegetables immediately.

4 To prepare the vegetables, place the reserved marinade in a saucepan large enough to take all the vegetables. Add 4 tbsp water and bring to the boil. Add the vegetables and simmer gently for 2–3 minutes.

5 To serve, place a fillet of fish on a heated plate. Spoon the vegetables over the fillet, and serve with a piece of lemon. This makes an excellent starter. For a more substantial meal, serve with Oriental noodles.
SERVES 6.

TIPS

- This is a very versatile dish. Replace the fish with deveined prawns, grilled for 3 minutes per side. Boned chicken breasts, cubed turkey, or strips of beef or pork can also replace the fish.

- The vegetables can be varied according to seasonal availability, although remember that using a variety of different coloured vegetables helps to make this an attractive dish. Options include cauliflower and broccoli florets, sliced courgettes, mushrooms and small pickling onions.

- Soy sauce has been used for centuries in Eastern cooking. It is made from fermented, cooked soybeans and wheat, which have been salted and into which a mould has been injected.

POACHED WHOLE FISH

Most kinds of whole fish, especially salmon trout, are excellent poached. This is a gentle method of cooking always using a court bouillon.

1 x approximately 2 kg ($4^1/_2$ lb) salmon trout, whole salmon, or any other large fish
cucumber, thinly sliced
lemon slices

COURT BOUILLON
water to cover fish
250 ml (8 fl oz) white wine
1 onion, peeled and sliced
1 large lemon, sliced
2 sticks celery, sliced
2 bay leaves, or 4 lemon leaves
1 bouquet garni (sprigs of parsley, sage and fennel or dill)
1 tsp salt
a few black peppercorns

1 Wash the fish and pat dry with absorbent paper. To work out the poaching time, measure the fish at the thickest point; allow 10 minutes of cooking time for every 2.5 cm (1 in). Start timing the cooking when the court bouillon starts to bubble again after the fish has been added.

2 Combine all the ingredients for the court bouillon in a large saucepan or fish kettle. Bring to the boil, and cook, uncovered, for 15 minutes.

3 Place the fish on a fish kettle trivet, or on a piece of foil folded over twice and gently lowered into the simmering liquid. Bring to a gentle simmer and cook for the calculated time.

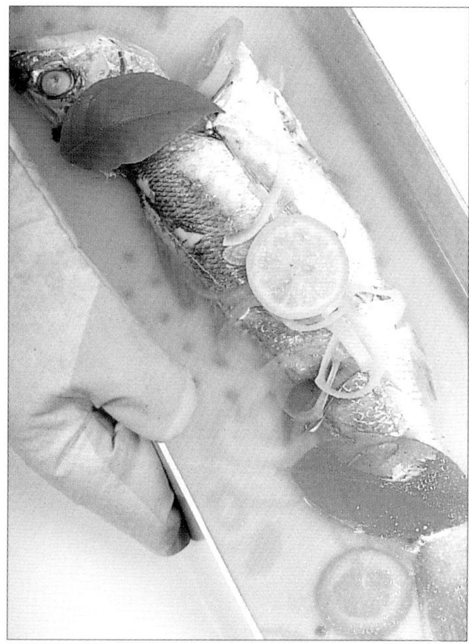

4 Remove from the heat and allow fish to cool completely in the liquid. Keep refrigerated or in a cool place. When cold, remove from the pan. Carefully remove all the skin, and discard the gills. If preferred, cut off and discard head.

5 With a pair of scissors, cut down the backbone and carefully ease out the bones.

6 Slide the boned whole fish very carefully onto a serving platter. Carefully wipe the platter clean. The fish can be served with the remaining bones intact (inform guests that you are doing so), or continue as follows to fillet.

7 To divide the fish into two fillets, cut horizontally down the easily visible centre line on the side of the fish facing uppermost on the platter. Ease the top fillet to one side of the platter. The backbone is now visible: snap the backbone at the head, then pull the bone out from the head to the tail. Replace the top fillet very carefully, and reshape the fish. Carefully clean the serving platter.

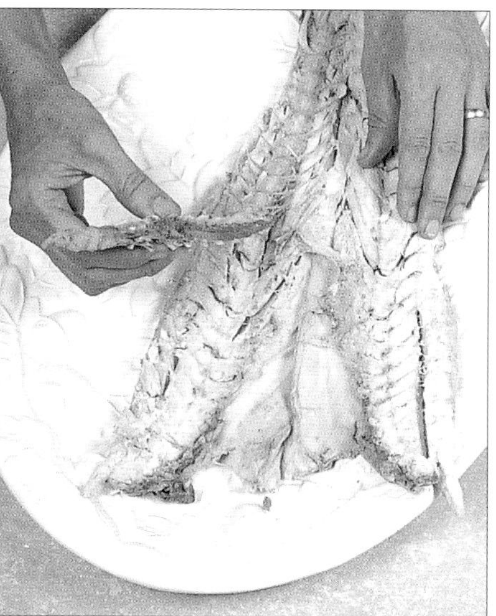

8 Cover the deboned fish with overlapping cucumber slices and garnish with lemon slices. The fish platter makes an excellent display on a buffet table. Serve fish cold with boiled new potatoes or potato salad, and a Hollandaise sauce (see p. 29) or homemade mayonnaise (see p. 61).
SERVES 6.

TIP

◆ To make a good sauce to serve with the fish, reduce the court bouillon by boiling until halved. Add 120 ml (4 fl oz) cream and thicken with a beurre manié – a paste made of 3 tbsp each butter and flour. Whisk well.

KEDGEREE

A light, meal-in-one dish composed of flakes of smoked fish, eggs and rice. Ideal as a supper dish, it is also perfect on a brunch menu.

500 g (18 oz) smoked haddock, fresh or frozen
250 ml (8 fl oz) water
120 ml (4 fl oz) white wine
1 onion, sliced in three
1 carrot, sliced
1 bay leaf
200 g (7 oz) rice
750 ml (1¼ pints) boiling water
3 extra-large eggs, hard-boiled
1 tbsp butter
1 tbsp oil
1 large onion, finely chopped
1 bunch of spring onions, chopped
1–2 tsp mild curry powder
2 tbsp cream
salt and freshly ground black pepper
2 tbsp chopped fresh parsley
1 tbsp finely chopped fresh dill

1 Place the haddock in a saucepan and add water and white wine. Add onion, carrot and bay leaf. If using fresh haddock, poach for 10 minutes; if using frozen, poach for 15–20 minutes, or until the fish is soft and flakes.

2 When the haddock is cooked, remove from liquid with a slotted spoon, and reserve 3 tbsp poaching liquid. Allow the fish to cool enough to handle, then remove the skin and flake with a fork. Set aside.

3 Place rice in a saucepan and add boiling water and 1 tsp salt. Boil until the rice is cooked, and the water has evaporated.

4 Dice the hard-boiled eggs, and set aside.

5 Pre-heat the butter and oil in a saucepan. Fry the onion and spring onions until soft, and then add the curry powder and fry for a further 3 minutes. Remove from the saucepan and set aside. Add the reserved poaching liquid and the cream to the saucepan, and de-glaze the pan.

6 In an ovenproof baking dish, combine fish, rice, egg, onion and curry mixture, seasoning, parsley and dill. Mix lightly with a fork – over-mixing will result in a mushy mixture. Pour the hot poaching liquid and cream from the pan over the top. If necessary, re-heat the kedgeree, covered, in the oven at 200 °C (400 °F/gas 6) for 15 minutes.

SERVES 4–6.

TIPS

- Any other smoked fish, e.g. mackerel or smoked trout, can replace the smoked haddock.
- Brown rice can be used instead of white rice if preferred.

GRILLED PRAWNS

Delicious with garlic and lemon butter.

6–8 large prawns or 10–12 small prawns per person

MARINADE
100 g (4 oz) butter
100 ml (3½ fl oz) oil
juice of 2 lemons
2 cloves garlic, crushed

GARLIC BUTTER
125 g (4½ oz) butter
2 cloves garlic, crushed
½ tsp salt
½ tsp freshly ground black pepper

LEMON BUTTER
125 g (4½ oz) butter
2 tbsp lemon juice
1 clove garlic, crushed (optional)
½ tsp salt
½ tsp white pepper

1 Prawns are usually purchased frozen. Soak in a bowl of cold water until just soft enough to handle. Devein by cutting down the back of the prawn with a pair of very sharp, pointed scissors, or a sharp knife. Lift the black vein with a sharp point, and discard. Rinse the prawn very briefly under cold running water. Set aside in an ovenproof dish.

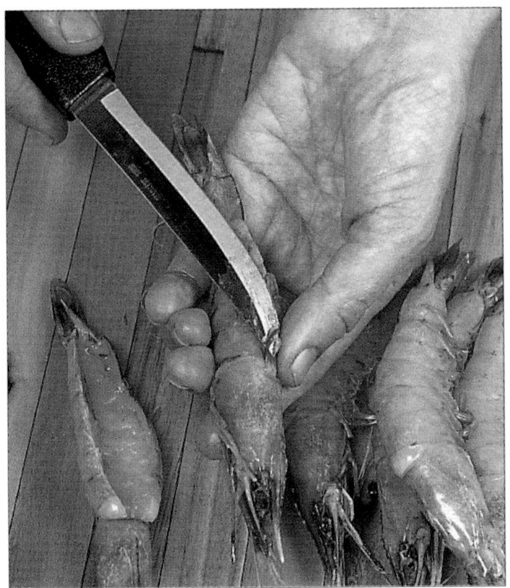

2 Combine all the ingredients for the marinade in a small saucepan. Place on the hob and allow to simmer but not to boil. Cool, and then pour over prawns. Marinate for 1 hour.

3 Pre-heat the grill. Remove the prawns from the marinade and place side-by-side, cut side up, in a grill pan. Brush with the remaining marinade. Grill approximately 6 cm (2½ in) from the heat source for 3–4 minutes per side. If the prawns are very small, grill for 2 minutes per side. Baste frequently with marinade. As soon as the shell changes colour, the prawns are ready. Do not overcook, as they become hard.

4 To make the garlic butter, melt the butter and combine with the remaining ingredients.

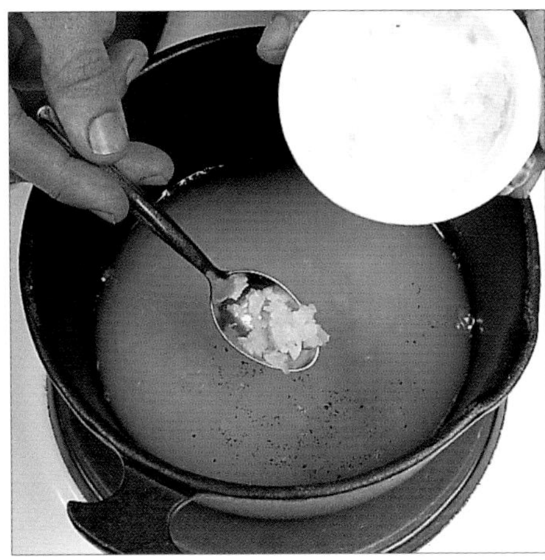

5 To make the lemon butter, melt the butter and combine with the remaining ingredients in a small serving dish.

6 Serve prawns straight from the oven on savoury rice, with the garlic and lemon butters.

TIP

- To make savoury rice, stir 2 tsp paprika, ½ tsp cayenne pepper, seasoning, 1 each chopped red and yellow pepper and 4 tbsp chopped parsley into a bowl of cooked, fluffy white rice.

DEEP-FRIED CALAMARI

Calamari requires either a quick cooking over high heat, or long, slow cooking; to achieve a tender and delicious result, I have chosen rapid deep-frying. The calamari either can be dredged with flour or coated in a batter before being deep-fried – it is a matter of personal preference, and you should select the method you require.

1 kg ($2^1/_4$ lb) cleaned calamari, or 1.5–2 kg ($3^1/_4$–$4^1/_2$ lb) uncleaned calamari

FLOUR COATING
125 g ($4^1/_2$ oz) plain flour
clean oil for deep-frying
salt
lemon wedges

BATTER COATING
125 g ($4^1/_2$ oz) plain flour
1 tsp baking powder
pinch of salt
1 large egg
1 tbsp oil
150 ml (5 fl oz) milk or water
clean oil for deep-frying
salt
lemon wedges

1 If the calamari has not been cleaned, cut off the head and tentacles and discard the head. Peel the purplish skin off the body and throw away. Pull out the transparent quills. Slice the tentacles and the body into rings. Dry well on absorbent paper.

2 If using a flour coating, preheat approximately 10 cm (4 in) oil, for deep-frying. Dip the calamari rings into the flour and shake off the excess.

3 Divide the calamari rings into 4 portions and fry one portion at a time, until the rings are golden on one side, then turn and fry the other side. Drain on absorbent paper, sprinkle with salt, and serve immediately with lemon wedges or Tartare sauce (see p. 42).

4 If using batter, sift flour, baking powder and salt into a mixing bowl. Combine egg, oil and milk or water in another bowl. Make a well in the centre of the dry ingredients, pour in the egg mixture, and stir with a wooden spoon until the batter is smooth.

5 Divide the calamari rings into 4 portions and fry one portion at a time. Drop the calamari rings into the batter, then remove with a fork, and place in approximately 10 cm (4 in) deep, pre-heated oil. Fry until golden and puffy. Drain on absorbent paper. Sprinkle lightly with salt, and serve immediately with lemon wedges or Tartare sauce (see p. 42).
SERVES 4 AS A MAIN MEAL, OR 6 AS A STARTER.

TIP

◆ Calamari can sometimes be very tough and chewy, but the following tip helps to soften it: cover the rings in milk and leave to stand for 1 hour, then pour off the milk, dry well with absorbent paper, and proceed with coating for frying.

CRAYFISH MAYONNAISE

Crayfish, otherwise known as rock lobster, is called the king of shellfish. If buying fresh crayfish, make sure that they are alive and moving.

1 crayfish per person
boiling water

MAYONNAISE
2 extra-large egg yolks
½ tsp mustard powder
½ tsp salt
pinch of white pepper
½ tsp sugar
250 ml (8 fl oz) sunflower or salad oil
1 tbsp vinegar or lemon juice
1 tbsp chopped fresh herbs (parsley, tarragon and dill)

1 First weigh the crayfish. Then place it on a board and, using one hand, hold it down firmly with a clean kitchen cloth. With the point of a large knife, pierce through the crayfish where the tail joins the body. The crayfish may continue to twitch because of the severed nerve endings.

2 Place the crayfish in rapidly boiling water and cook for 5 minutes per 450 g (1 lb). Do not overcook. Remove from the water and cool enough to handle.

3 Using a sharp knife, cut in half lengthwise. Remove the intestinal vein that runs the length of the crayfish, and the soft matter in the body and top of the head. (The remaining cooked crayfish can be tightly wrapped and then refrigerated in the coldest part of the refrigerator for up to 24 hours.)

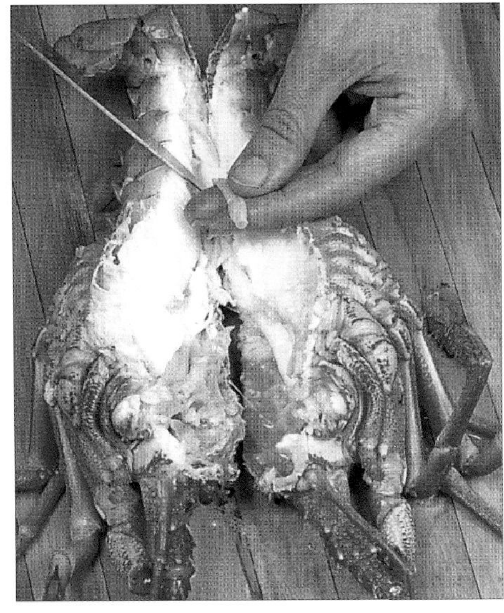

4 Remove the crayfish flesh gently so as not to damage the shells, and cut into blocks and set aside. Reserve the halved shells.

5 To prepare the mayonnaise, have all the ingredients at room temperature. Place the egg yolks, mustard powder, seasoning and sugar in the bowl of a food processor. Using the metal blade, mix thoroughly until smooth.

6 Keep the processor running while you add the oil through the feeder in a slow, steady stream. Finally add vinegar or lemon juice and mix well. Fold in fresh herbs.

7 To serve, either combine the crayfish flesh with some mayonnaise and arrange on a plate decorated with the crayfish shells, or return the crayfish flesh to the shell halves, spoon mayonnaise over the top, and arrange the crayfish halves on a plate. Garnish with spring onions, lettuce leaves, cocktail tomatoes and hard-boiled egg slices. Chill, and serve with extra mayonnaise.

TIP

◆ Crayfish are excellent when barbecued – brush frequently with melted butter and cook for about 10 minutes, turning once. Serve immediately.

STUFFED MUSSELS

The large half-shell, black mussels available fresh or frozen at your local fishmonger or supermarket are perfect for this dish.

- 1 kg (2¼ lb) half-shell black mussels, fresh or frozen
- 125 g (4½ oz) fresh white breadcrumbs
- 125 g (4½ oz) butter
- 4 spring onions, finely chopped
- 2 cloves garlic, peeled and very finely chopped
- 2 tbsp very finely chopped fresh parsley
- 1 tbsp very finely chopped fresh dill
- 2 tbsp white wine
- a dash of Tabasco sauce
- salt and freshly ground black pepper
- lemon slices
- extra sprigs of fresh dill to garnish

1 If using fresh mussels, scrub under cold water and remove the stringy 'beard'. Steam in a large saucepan for about 5 minutes, then discard any that do not open. Discard half the shell. If using frozen mussels, do not defrost. Arrange mussels on a baking sheet.

2 Combine breadcrumbs, butter, spring onions, garlic, parsley, dill, wine, Tabasco and seasoning for 2 minutes in a food processor fitted with metal blade.

3 If using fresh mussels, make sure that they have cooled completely. Spread about 2 tsp of the stuffing mixture over each mussel, being careful not to damage the delicate flesh.

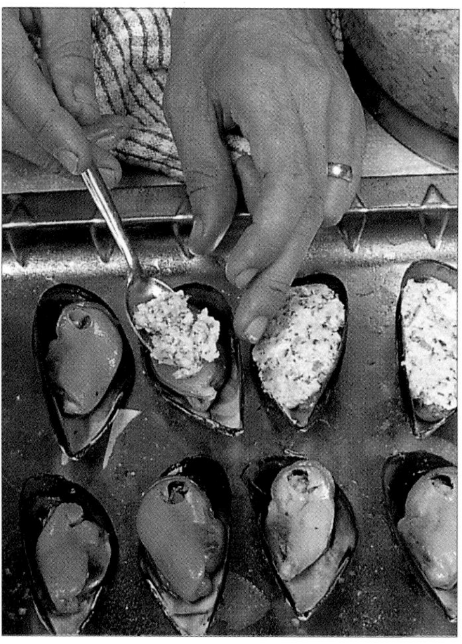

4 Place under a pre-heated grill, and grill for 3–5 minutes, until the breadcrumbs are golden and the butter is melted. Place on individual, heated serving dishes, or a large heated platter. Garnish with lemon halves and sprigs of dill. Serve with a dry white wine.

SERVES 4–6 AS A STARTER, OR 3 AS A MAIN MEAL.

TIPS

◆ Do not use canned mussels for this dish. They are too small to be stuffed successfully, and the brine in the can detracts from the flavour.

◆ Mussels are found worldwide and come in a variety of colours. Any common large mussel can be used for this dish, but it is no good stuffing the small ones – they are simply not as tasty, and there is very little area to stuff.

◆ Frozen half-shell mussels are ideal as they are ready-cleaned and pre-steamed. Do not defrost, simply spread with stuffing and grill.

30-MINUTE CHICKEN CURRY

I learnt how to make this tasty dish at a course on Sri Lankan cooking I attended in Hong Kong. In just under one hour, a meal of dinner party standard is ready to be served.

1.5 kg ($3\frac{1}{4}$ lb) chicken thighs
2 tsp salt
5 cloves
5 cardamoms
2 tsp curry powder
1–2 tsp chilli powder
$\frac{1}{2}$ tsp turmeric
1 tbsp ground coriander
2 tsp paprika
500 ml (17 fl oz) boiling water
100 g (4 oz) desiccated coconut
3 tbsp oil
1 large onion, finely chopped
2 cm ($\frac{3}{4}$ in) piece of fresh ginger, peeled and finely grated
3 cloves garlic, crushed
4 cm ($1\frac{1}{2}$ in) piece of lemon grass
4 red tomatoes, peeled and chopped
3 bay leaves
1 stick of cinnamon
2 green chillies

1 Remove skin from chicken. Combine salt, cloves, cardamoms, curry powder, chilli powder, turmeric, coriander and paprika. Rub into chicken and set aside for at least 5 minutes, or cover and refrigerate overnight to improve flavour.

2 Pour boiling water over coconut and set aside to swell. Meanwhile, pre-heat oil in pan. Add onion and fry until light brown. Add ginger, garlic, lemon grass, tomatoes, bay leaves and cinnamon. Sauté for a few minutes.

3 Slice chillies in half and remove the seeds, which are the hot and spicy part. Cut chillies into thin slivers and add to onion mixture. Be careful, chillies are very hot: do not rub your eyes after handling chilli, and wash your hands carefully. It may be helpful to wear rubber gloves.

4 Add the chicken to the onion mixture. Sauté for a few minutes.

5 Strain the coconut milk by pouring the steeped coconut into a clean cloth placed over a bowl. Squeeze out all the coconut milk into the bowl, and discard the desiccated coconut. Add the coconut milk to the chicken. Cover and simmer for 30 minutes, stirring occasionally. Check the seasoning. Serve with dhal (lentils) or rice, and a selection of tasty sambals, and note that the gravy is not a thick one.
SERVES 4–6.

TIPS

- Curry always tastes better if made the day before eating.
- Serve with these sambals:
  - banana slices dipped in fresh lemon juice and rolled in desiccated coconut.
  - thick Greek yoghurt with grated cucumber and a hint of garlic.
  - roasted peanuts mixed with seedless raisins and sultanas.
  - finely chopped onion, green and red pepper, and skinned and chopped tomato.

CHICKEN FLORENTINE

This dish can be whipped up quickly, and is excellent for using up leftover chicken or turkey.

500 g (18 oz) fresh spinach
1 tsp ground nutmeg
500 g (18 oz) chicken breast fillets
500 ml (17 fl oz) chicken stock
3 tbsp butter
3 tbsp oil
1 onion, finely chopped
300 g (11 oz) button mushrooms, sliced
1–2 tsp curry paste (optional)
3 tbsp flour
250 ml (8 fl oz) milk
salt and freshly ground black pepper
25 g (1 oz) freshly grated breadcrumbs
2 tbsp Parmesan cheese

1 Wash spinach well in plenty of salted water. Tear spinach from stalks and place leaves in a pan. Add 100 ml (3½ fl oz) water and cook for 5 minutes. Drain very well, then chop with a sharp knife or in a food processor. Add nutmeg. Place a layer of spinach in the bottom of an oval 18 x 28 cm (7 x 11 in) baking dish.

2 Poach chicken in boiling chicken stock for 4 minutes. Drain and reserve 250 ml (8 fl oz) stock for sauce. Slice chicken into slivers and place on top of spinach.

3 To make sauce, melt together butter and oil, add onion and gently fry until soft. Add mushrooms and curry paste, if using, and sauté for a few minutes.

4 Stir flour into butter and mushroom mixture with a wooden spoon.

5 Add milk and reserved chicken stock. Stir over medium heat until sauce is cooked and thickened, then add seasoning.

6 Pour sauce over chicken. Combine breadcrumbs and Parmesan cheese and top sauce with this mixture. Bake at 180 °C (350 °F/gas 4) for 45 minutes, until heated through and breadcrumbs are golden brown. Serve with baked potatoes and a salad.
SERVES 4.

TIPS

◆ If you need this dish at lightning speed, use frozen spinach and replace sauce with a can of mushroom soup. Defrost spinach, squeeze out all excess moisture and place in a baking dish. Dilute soup with 250 ml (8 fl oz) milk, heat gently, stirring until soup is smooth, then pour over chicken. Top with crumbs and bake in the oven at 180 °C (350 °F/gas 4) for 45 minutes.

◆ This dish is an excellent way to use up leftover roast chicken or turkey. If you are doing so, replace 500 ml (17 fl oz) chicken stock with 250 ml (8 fl oz) chicken stock made with a stock cube. Omit step 2 and instead simply slice the leftover meat into slivers and place on top of spinach.

ROAST DUCK WITH ORANGE SAUCE

Duck has more fat than chicken or turkey but less meat. Allow 350–500 g (12–18 oz) per person. The citrus flavour of the orange sauce marries well with the richness of the duck.

1 x 2 kg (4½ lb) duck
salt and freshly ground black pepper

ORANGE SAUCE
75 g (3 oz) sugar
4 tbsp water
250 ml (8 fl oz) freshly squeezed orange juice
5 tsp grated orange rind
3 tbsp chunky orange marmalade*
4 tbsp brandy

1 Wipe duck inside and out with a damp cloth. Prick skin all over, to allow the fat to drain out of duck. Sprinkle generously with salt and pepper. The salt helps to crisp the skin.

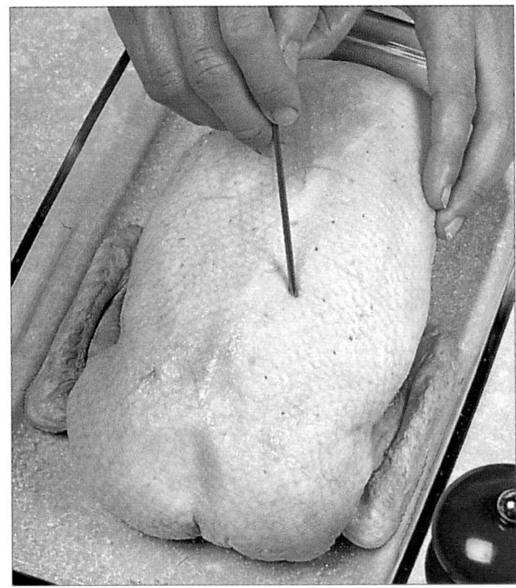

2 Place breast-side up in a roasting tin, and bake at 180 °C (350 °F/gas 4) for 2 hours. Allow 30 minutes for every 500 g (18 oz). The oven temperature may be reduced to 160 °C (325 °F/gas 3) after 1 hour. The duck must rest for 15 minutes in the warming drawer before carving.

3 To make the sauce, dissolve sugar in the water in a heavy-based saucepan. Stir over low heat until the sugar dissolves, then boil, without stirring, until the mixture changes to a golden colour.

4 Add orange juice, rind, marmalade and brandy. Simmer until slightly reduced. Pour over the roast duck or serve in a gravy boat. Serve duck in the traditional way, accompanied by roast or boiled potatoes, green peas and baby carrots and gravy.
SERVES 4.

TIPS

* Replace orange marmalade with apricot jam if preferred.

◆ Grand Marnier is a sweet, citrus-based liqueur. It is an ideal substitute for the brandy.

◆ For ease of carving, buy two smaller ducks for 4 people, allowing half a duck per person.

◆ To carve a duck, snip the skin between the legs and body with sharp kitchen scissors in preparation for carving the breast meat. Slice under the wing joints through the breast meat to the bone. Cut off the duck wings, which are normally discarded. Cutting straight down, carve thin slices of breast meat working back across the duck breast. Remove the legs by forcing the knife into the joint and severing the leg. Cut the legs in half through the joint.

◆ For the best results when carving, always use a perfectly sharpened carving knife and a carving fork.

ROAST TURKEY WITH MACADAMIA BUTTER

Roast turkey has reigned over the English table since the seventeenth century, and is the perfect bird for a celebration. Macadamia butter keeps the breast beautifully moist, and the stuffing is a delicious complement.

1 x 6 kg (13½ lb) turkey
250 ml (8 fl oz) water
oil

MACADAMIA BUTTER
100 g (4 oz) macadamia nuts
2 tsp oil
150 g (5 oz) softened butter
2 cloves garlic, crushed
2 tbsp chopped fresh parsley

BACON, MUSHROOM AND ROSEMARY STUFFING
8 rashers fatty streaky bacon
2 onions, chopped
250 g (9 oz) mushrooms, sliced
2 tbsp chopped fresh rosemary
4 sticks celery, chopped
250 g (9 oz) fresh breadcrumbs
salt and freshly ground black pepper

1 Remove neck and giblets from turkey. Rinse with cold water and pat dry inside and out. Very carefully loosen skin over breast and tops of legs using fingers, without tearing the skin.

2 To make the macadamia butter, toast the nuts in oil in a frying pan on the hob. Stir constantly, watching carefully, as nuts burn very quickly.

3 Combine nuts, butter, garlic and parsley in a food processor and process until smooth. Chill until firm. Push butter under loosened skin, again taking care not to break skin.

4 To prepare stuffing, cook bacon in pan until crisp. Remove and cut into small pieces. Add onions, mushrooms, rosemary and celery to pan and fry in bacon fat for a few minutes – add more oil if needed. Remove from heat. Stir in crumbs, bacon and seasoning.

5 Allow stuffing to cool completely before filling the turkey cavity just before roasting. Place in roasting tin and add water. Brush evenly with oil. Bake in a pre-heated oven at 180 °C (350 °F/gas 4) for 30 minutes, then reduce temperature to 160 °C (325 °F/gas 3) and roast for approximately 3½ hours. After 1 hour, cover turkey with foil so skin does not darken too much. Turkey is ready when it is golden brown and the juices run clear when pierced in the drumstick joint with a fork. Serve with gravy, roast potatoes, Brussels sprouts and glazed carrots.
SERVES 6–8.

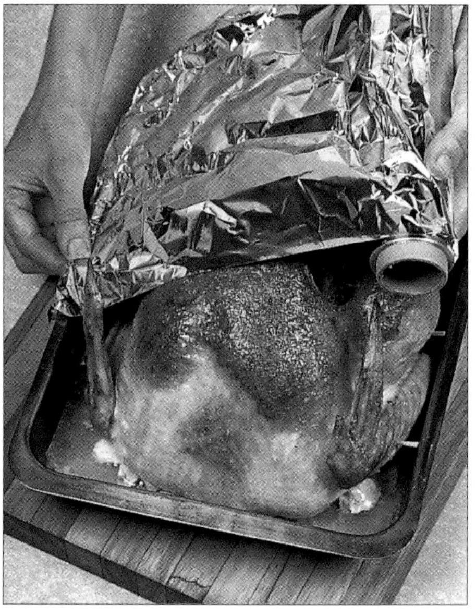

TIP

◆ To truss a turkey, place turkey breast-side up. Neatly bring legs close to breast and tuck wings in. Cut a long piece of butcher's string. Take string across neck end of the breast, over wings, and cross string beneath turkey. Bring string up and back over legs, and then tie the drumsticks and parson's nose together.

CHICKEN SATE STICKS

Indonesian satés make an excellent starter, and are delicious barbecued.

8 chicken breasts
24 wooden kebab sticks

MARINADE
150 ml (5 fl oz) olive oil
100 ml ($3^1/_2$ fl oz) fresh lemon juice
2 cloves garlic, crushed
2 tsp garam masala, or curry powder
pinch of cayenne pepper
$^1/_2$ tsp ground ginger
salt and freshly ground black pepper
1 tbsp finely chopped fresh coriander
sesame seeds

PEANUT SAUCE
100 g (4 oz) chunky peanut butter
1 tbsp fresh lemon juice
1 clove garlic, crushed
1 tsp caster sugar
2 tbsp soy sauce
1 tsp Tabasco sauce
1–2 tbsp medium cream sherry
120 ml (4 fl oz) single cream

1 Cut each chicken breast into 3 long strips.

2 To make marinade, combine all ingredients except sesame seeds in a non-metallic dish. Place chicken strips in marinade, stirring well and coating thoroughly. Cover and leave in the refrigerator overnight, or for at least 3 hours.

3 Remove strips from marinade and, starting from narrowest end of each strip, loop chicken onto sticks in a wavy pattern. Dip into sesame seeds.

4 Place satés over hot coals or under grill until golden brown, basting frequently with marinade. They cook very quickly – about 3 minutes per side.

5 To make peanut sauce, combine all ingredients except sherry and cream in a small saucepan. Cook over low heat, stirring constantly until smooth. Reduce heat, add sherry and cream, and heat through. Pour into a small dish and serve separately. Serve satés with tomato and spring onion garnish, a sprig of coriander, and finger bowls.
SERVES 6–8.

TIPS

◆ For a peanut sauce with more bite, add 1–2 tsp chilli powder.

◆ The sauce may be prepared in advance, covered tightly and refrigerated for up to 2 days.

◆ It is a good idea to soak the kebab sticks in water for 2 hours before use. This prevents them from burning.

◆ For an interesting variation, make up a selection of chicken, beef and pork saté sticks. Marinate strips of beef and pork in the same way as the chicken, and proceed with step 2 as above.

SOUTHERN FRIED CHICKEN

The secret of this succulent, delicious chicken lies in the double cooking – first it is cooked in a pressure cooker to keep it moist, then in a deep-fryer to get a tasty, crispy crust.

1 kg (2¼ lb) chicken pieces
water
salt and freshly ground black pepper
125 g (4½ oz) plain flour
1 tsp paprika
1 tsp garlic salt
1 tsp onion salt
1 tsp mixed dried herbs
1 extra-large egg
85 ml (3 fl oz) milk
2 tbsp lemon juice
sunflower oil for frying

1 Place the chicken pieces in a pressure cooker. Cover with water and season with salt and pepper. Cook on full steam for 10 minutes. Allow to cool, then remove the chicken from the pressure cooker.

2 Combine the flour, paprika, garlic salt, onion salt and mixed herbs in a flat dish. Beat together the egg, milk and lemon juice, and place in a separate, non-metallic flat dish.

3 Dip the chicken in the egg mixture and then in the seasoned flour. For a crisper, heavier crust, first lightly dust the chicken pieces with the seasoned flour, then dip the chicken pieces in the egg mixture, and then coat once more with seasoned flour.

4 Stand the chicken in the refrigerator for 30 minutes to set the coating before frying (this prevents the coating from falling off during frying).

5 Deep-fry in pre-heated oil until golden brown, then turn and fry on other side. Serve immediately with chips or baked potatoes, peas and a crisp salad.
SERVES 4–6.

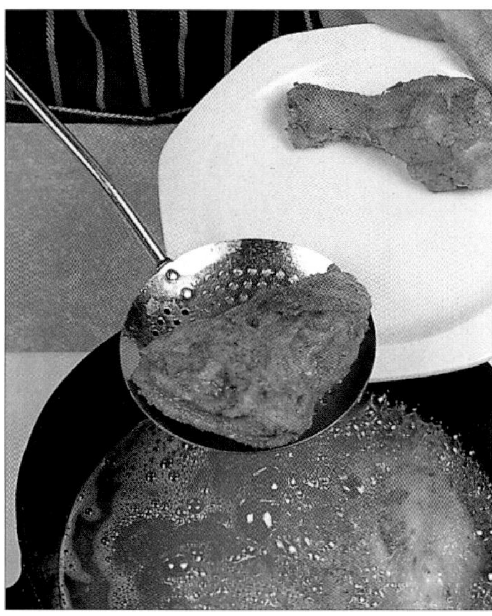

TIPS

◆ This chicken dish can be made ahead: prepare up to the end of step 4, then cover well and refrigerate or freeze.

◆ For a spicier coating, add 1 tsp peri-peri to flour.

◆ Deep-frying can be hazardous as the temperature of the hot oil is about 190 °C (375 °F), and the following precautions should always be taken:
- Never overfill the pan with oil. It should not be more than half full.
- If the oil happens to boil over, turn off the heat immediately and cover the pan with a lid or heavy baking sheet.
- If you are using a deep-frying pan, a wire basket is recommended for lowering and removing the food.

FRENCH ROAST CHICKEN

A delicious, succulent roast chicken with a surprise filling of spinach and feta cheese.

1 x 1.5 kg (3¼ lb) chicken
a little oil
salt and freshly ground black pepper
250 ml (8 fl oz) chicken stock

STUFFING
5 tsp oil
5 tsp butter
1 onion, finely chopped
2 spring onions, finely chopped
1 clove garlic, crushed
100 g (4 oz) washed and finely chopped fresh spinach
125 g (4½ oz) feta cheese, crumbled
1 x 2 cm (¾ in) thick slice of brown bread, crusts removed and grated
3 tbsp chopped pecan nuts
1 tsp ground nutmeg

1 Working from the neck, gently loosen the skin over the chicken breast, taking care not to tear it.

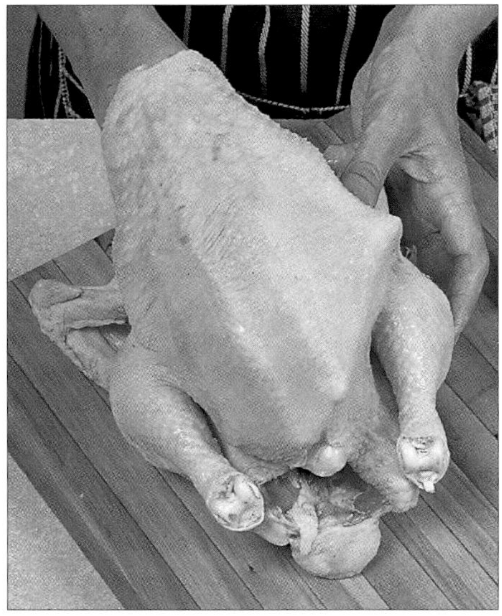

2 To make stuffing, heat oil and butter. Add onion and spring onions. Fry until soft and golden. Add garlic and spinach and fry until soft. Add cheese, breadcrumbs, nuts and nutmeg. Cool.

3 Place cooled stuffing in cavity beneath loosened skin. Secure with cocktail sticks.

4 Place chicken, uncovered, in roasting tin. Brush lightly with oil and seasoning. Pour stock around bird. Roast at 160 °C (325 °F/gas 3) for 1½ hours.

5 Baste the chicken every 30 minutes with the pan juices. Do not turn chicken as this will damage the breast. If the skin browns too quickly, cover loosely with foil. Rest for 15 minutes in warming drawer before carving.

6 To make gravy, thicken pan juices on stove top with 1 tbsp flour. Stir constantly with a wooden spoon, if necessary adding more liquid such as white wine, chicken stock or water. Reduce, then pour into a gravy boat, and serve with chicken. Serve with roast potatoes and seasonal vegetables.
SERVES 4–6.

TIPS

- Remember to remove cocktail sticks before serving!
- Frozen spinach may be used if fresh is unavailable. Defrost and squeeze out excess moisture before frying.
- This recipe also makes an excellent, succulent plain roast chicken. Simply leave out the stuffing, brush the chicken with oil, season with salt and freshly ground black pepper, and add 250 ml (8 fl oz) chicken stock to the roasting tin. Roast at 180 °C (350 °F/gas 4) for 1¼ hours.

CHICKEN STIR-FRY WITH FRIED RICE

A wholesome meal packed with a selection of crunchy vegetables.

4 tbsp soy sauce
1 tbsp dry sherry
1 tbsp cornflour
2 tsp sugar
1 clove garlic, crushed
2 tsp finely grated fresh ginger, or 1 tsp ground ginger
575 g (1¼ lb) skinless chicken breast fillets, thinly sliced
3 tbsp oil
575 g (1¼ lb) vegetables such as cauliflower florets, bean sprouts, sliced carrots, spring onions, shredded cabbage, red and green peppers, and sugar snap peas
125 g (4½ oz) mushrooms, sliced
salt and freshly ground black pepper

FRIED RICE
200 g (7 oz) rice
750 ml (1¼ pints) water
salt
125 g (4½ oz) rindless streaky bacon
2 eggs, lightly beaten
2 tbsp oil
3 tbsp chopped spring onion
1 tbsp soy sauce

1 Mix the soy sauce, sherry, cornflour, sugar, garlic and ginger in a bowl. Add the chicken pieces, and toss well to cover all the pieces. Leave to stand for 30 minutes.

2 Heat oil and stir-fry chicken in the marinade for 4 minutes. Add vegetables and stir-fry for a further 3–5 minutes. Season.

3 To make fried rice, cook rice in water with a little salt until just tender and water has evaporated. Meanwhile, fry bacon in its own fat, until crisp. Cool and break into bite-sized pieces.

4 Pour the eggs into the bacon fat and scramble slowly over gentle heat until set but not hard. Remove from the pan. Cool and break up into small pieces.

5 Add 2 tbsp oil to the pan, add the rice and stir over medium heat until coated with oil. Add the bacon, scrambled egg, spring onion and soy sauce. Heat through. Top with the stir-fried chicken and vegetables, and serve.
SERVES 6.

TIPS

◆ This recipe is an excellent way of using up leftover odds and ends of vegetables.

◆ Chicken can also be replaced by thin strips of beef or pork.

◆ If desired, the streaky bacon can be omitted from the recipe: scramble the egg in 1 tbsp pre-heated cooking oil.

◆ Sprinkle with sesame seeds just before serving, to add crunch.

◆ For a vegetarian meal, replace the chicken with tofu (soy bean curd). Tofu has little flavour, but absorbs other flavours, making it ideal for stir-fries. Cut 250 g (9 oz) tofu into blocks and proceed as above with step 1.

CHICKEN JAMBALAYA

This is an adaptation of a Creole dish. It is flavoursome, colourful and slightly spicy, and needs just a green salad as an accompaniment.

3 tbsp oil
6 chicken thighs, skinned
4 chicken drumsticks
1 chorizo sausage, sliced
1 large onion, chopped
1–2 red chillies, seeded and sliced
1 each red and green pepper, seeded and chopped
1 large carrot, sliced into rings
2 cloves garlic, crushed
400 g (14 oz) rice
500 ml (17 fl oz) chicken stock
120 ml (4 fl oz) dry white wine
1 tsp dried basil, or 1 tbsp chopped fresh basil
1 tsp dried oregano, or 1 tbsp chopped fresh oregano
5 tsp chopped fresh parsley
1 x 400 g can peeled tomatoes, sliced and juice reserved
1 tsp sugar
1 tsp chilli powder
few drops of Tabasco sauce
salt and freshly ground black pepper

1 Heat the oil in a large, heavy-based saucepan with a lid. Brown the chicken and chorizo sausage. Remove with a slotted spoon and set aside.

2 Add onion to pan and allow to soften and change in colour. Add chillies, peppers, carrot and garlic. Sauté until soft.

3 Add rice to pan and stir-fry until well coated in oil.

4 Stir in the chicken stock, white wine, herbs, tomatoes with juice, and sugar.

5 Return the chicken and sausage to the pan. Add the chilli powder and Tabasco. Bring to the boil, cover and simmer for 25 minutes, until the rice is tender and the liquid has been absorbed.

6 Take care that it does not catch at the bottom, but don't stir as this will make the rice mushy. Check the seasoning, and serve with a green salad.
SERVES 6.

TIPS

◆ Chorizo, a spicy Mediterranean sausage, is available from speciality stores or delicatessens. If it is unavailable, use any other spicy sausage.

◆ The seeds of chillies are very hot and should be removed, together with the ribs, before they are cooked.

◆ Chillies need to be handled with great care as they can burn your eyes or skin if they get into contact with them. Wash your hands and all surfaces after handling them, do not touch your face, and if you don't find them too clumsy, consider wearing rubber gloves while handling chillies.

◆ The longer chillies are cooked, the hotter they taste.

◆ To reduce the heat of chillies, soak them for 1 hour in 3 parts mild vinegar to 1 part salt.

◆ Choose red or green peppers that have a bright colour and no soft spots. They should be firm and not wrinkled. The ribs of the peppers should be removed together with the seeds.

COQ AU VIN

A classic French dish. Remember, the better the wine, the better the dish will taste.

5 tsp butter
1 tbsp olive oil
200 g (7 oz) rindless streaky bacon
1 large chicken, jointed
2 tbsp brandy
12 pickling onions
4 sticks soup celery, sliced
300 g (11 oz) button mushrooms
1 clove garlic, crushed
1 large bouquet garni (parsley, thyme, celery leaves and bay leaf)
salt and freshly ground black pepper
750 ml ($1\frac{1}{4}$ pints) good red wine
5 tsp butter
5 tsp flour

1 Pre-heat 5 tsp butter and olive oil in a large casserole with a lid. Add the bacon and fry until crisp. Remove from the dish with a slotted spoon and set aside.

2 Brown the chicken in oil. Break the bacon into pieces and return to the casserole. Add pre-heated brandy to the dish and flame, shaking the dish until the flames have disappeared. Remove the chicken from the dish.

3 Add the onions, celery, mushrooms and garlic to the dish. Stir-fry for 3–5 minutes. Add bouquet garni and seasoning.

4 Return the chicken to the casserole and add the wine. Cover and bake at 180 °C (350 °F/gas 4) for 1 hour.

5 Mix 5 tsp butter with flour to form a smooth paste (this will make a beurre manié, which is the French term for kneaded butter, added at the end of cooking to thicken the consistency). Remove casserole lid and discard bouquet garni. Add the beurre manié and stir through on the hob. Serve with boiled potatoes.
SERVES 4–6.

TIPS

◆ A bouquet garni is a bunch of herbs used for flavouring casseroles, stocks and soups: the herbs are tied in a bundle or in a muslin bag with a long string for easy removal before serving.

◆ Poultry is particularly susceptible to salmonella contamination which can cause food poisoning. Follow these precautions:
- Chill the poultry sufficiently when storing.
- Handle poultry with clean hands and wash hands after handling poultry.
- Defrost the frozen poultry completely before cooking.
- Stuff the poultry just prior to roasting, instead of a long time before cooking.

◆ A good-sized chicken should be cut into about 10 portions: use a sharp knife or sharp kitchen scissors. Cut the legs from the body and halve at the knee joint, sever the wings from the body, cut across the rib cage to separate the breast from the back half of the body, then cut the breast in half lengthwise through the breastbone, and halve the back by cutting through the backbone.

CHICKEN PIE WITH HIGH-FIBRE PASTRY

This is a traditional old favourite with a modern adaptation – high fibre pastry. This very versatile, wholesome pastry can be used for any savoury dish, or add 1–2 tbsp caster sugar to make a sweet dough.

FILLING
1 x 1.5 kg (3¼ lb) chicken
water
1 onion studded with 3 cloves
1 carrot, sliced
1 stick soup celery, sliced and leaves retained
1 bay leaf
1 tbsp chopped fresh tarragon, or 1 tsp dried tarragon
4 tbsp butter
6 leeks, white part only, sliced
1 clove garlic, crushed
250 g (9 oz) button mushrooms, sliced
4 tbsp plain flour
375 ml (13 fl oz) reserved chicken stock
1 tbsp sago
100 ml (3½ fl oz) single cream
2 tbsp medium sherry
½ tsp ground nutmeg
1 tsp salt
freshly ground black pepper

HIGH-FIBRE PASTRY
100 g (4 oz) plain flour
1 tsp salt
1 tsp baking powder
100 g (4 oz) wholemeal flour
25 g (1 oz) digestive bran
100 g (4 oz) butter, cut into blocks
1 egg yolk
approximately 2–3 tbsp cold water
1 egg, beaten, for brushing over pastry
1 tbsp sesame seeds to sprinkle over pastry (optional)

1 Place the chicken in a large pan and add cold water to cover. Then add onion, carrot, celery, bay leaf and tarragon, and simmer for 45–60 minutes, until the chicken is tender.

2 Remove chicken from stock, and cool until it can be handled. Remove all skin and bones and set meat aside. Return bones to stock and boil to reduce stock until halved, making it rich and flavoursome.

3 Melt butter in a saucepan. Add leeks, fry until soft, then add garlic. Add sliced mushrooms, and fry until soft. Add flour, and stir to form a roux.

4 Add reserved stock, and stir constantly until the sauce is smooth and thickened. Add sago, cream, sherry, nutmeg, salt and pepper.

5 Optional extras like 125 g (4½ oz) cubed ham, whole kernel corn or peas can be added now. Stir in chicken. Pour into a 28 x 18 x 4 cm (11 x 7 x 1½ in) pie dish. Place an upturned ceramic egg cup in the centre of the chicken mixture as a support to prevent the pastry from sinking.

6 To make the pastry, sift the plain flour, salt and baking powder into a mixing bowl. Add the wholemeal flour and bran, and combine. Rub in the butter with your fingertips. Combine the egg yolk and water and add half to the flour-butter mixture, mixing with a round-bladed knife – add more liquid if necessary. Gather the dough together and place it on a lightly floured surface.

7 Roll out into a rectangle slightly larger than the pie dish. Wet edges of the dish. Roll pastry up over a rolling pin and place over filling in the pie dish, pressing down the edges. Using a sharp knife, cut a slit in the pastry to allow steam to escape. Cut decorative leaves out of remaining pastry, and press onto the top of pie. Brush the top with beaten egg and sprinkle with sesame seeds.

8 Place pie dish on baking sheet. Bake at 200 °C (400 °F/gas 6) for 20–30 minutes, until golden brown. Serve with a salad.
SERVES 4–6.

TASTY MINCE ROLL

Minced meat is an excellent standby, and can be turned quickly and economically into a roll with a surprise filling of cheese.

1 large onion, finely chopped
5 tsp oil
1 large clove garlic, crushed
1 kg (2¼ lb) lean beef mince
2 tbsp finely chopped fresh parsley
2 tsp salt
2 eggs, lightly beaten
4 cm (1½ in) thick slice of brown bread, crusts removed, grated
1 tsp mixed dried herbs, or 1 tbsp finely chopped fresh herbs
2 tsp soy sauce
150 g (5 oz) grated Cheddar cheese

RED PEPPER SAUCE
2 sweet red peppers, seeded and diced
1 small onion, finely chopped
5 tsp oil
1 clove garlic, crushed
1 tbsp tomato paste
450 ml (15 fl oz) chicken stock
4 tbsp white wine
salt and freshly ground black pepper
1 tsp sugar

1 Fry onion in oil until soft and golden brown. Add garlic and fry for a further minute. Set aside.

2 Combine mince, parsley, salt, eggs, breadcrumbs, herbs and soy sauce in a bowl.

3 Place a large piece of cling film (about 50 cm (20 in) long) on a flat surface. Spread the mince onto the cling film in a rectangle measuring approximately 30 x 40 cm (12 x 16 in). Do not press the mince out too thinly. Pat flat with hands, making sure that the edges are neatened.

4 Spread mince with a layer of cooled onion and garlic mixture. Top with grated cheese.

5 Lifting the cling film at the longer end, roll the mince rectangle up as you would a Swiss roll. Using two spatulas, lift the mince roll into an ovenproof dish. Bake at 160 °C (325 °F/gas 3) for 45–60 minutes.

6 To make the Red Pepper Sauce, fry the peppers and onion in oil. Add garlic and fry for a further minute. Add tomato paste, stock, wine, seasoning and sugar. Simmer for 15–30 minutes, until the peppers are tender.

7 Cool slightly, place in a blender and process until smooth, or purée by pressing through a sieve with a wooden spoon. Serve the mince roll with pasta of your choice, a selection of fresh vegetables and piping hot Red Pepper Sauce.
SERVES 4–6.

TIP

◆Replace the Cheddar cheese with mozzarella cheese if desired, and 300 g (11 oz) sliced button mushrooms fried with the onion and garlic in step 1 can either replace the cheese or be a tasty addition to the filling.

TAMALE PIE

Based on the original tamale, this Tex-Mex dish is hot and spicy, and an excellent dish for a buffet.

1 large onion, chopped
2 tbsp oil
1 each red and green pepper, seeded and diced
1 kg (2¼ lb) lean beef mince
250 ml (8 fl oz) tomato purée
1 x 410 g can whole kernel corn
100 g (4 oz) stuffed olives, sliced
1 tbsp ground cumin
1 tbsp cocoa powder*
1 tbsp ground allspice
3–4 tsp chilli powder, or to taste
4 tsp Worcestershire sauce
1 tsp Tabasco sauce

TOPPING
125 g (4½ oz) plain flour
125 g (4½ oz) polenta or yellow maize meal
2 tbsp caster sugar
2 tsp baking powder
3 tbsp butter, melted
200 ml (7 fl oz) milk
1 large egg, beaten
50 g (2 oz) Cheddar cheese, grated
2 tbsp red chillies, seeded and finely chopped

1 In a large flameproof casserole, sauté onion in oil until soft and golden brown. Add peppers and sauté until soft.

2 Add mince, and brown. Add the remaining ingredients and simmer for 10 minutes, stirring occasionally. If time permits, cover tightly and refrigerate overnight – this allows the flavours to develop and mingle.

3 To make the topping, combine the flour, polenta or maize meal, sugar and baking powder in a mixing bowl.

4 Mix butter, milk and egg, and add to the flour mixture. Mix to form a stiff batter, then stir in the cheese and chillies.

5 Spoon mounds of the batter to form dumplings around the edge of the casserole. Bake at 200 °C (400 °F/gas 6) for about 10 minutes, then reduce to 180 °C (350 °F/gas 4) and bake for a further 30 minutes.

SERVES 6.

TIPS

* Cocoa powder imparts an interesting flavour and a lovely deep, dark brown colour.

◆ For convenience, grate cheese and freeze it in an airtight container for up to 1 month. Do not defrost before using.

BEEF WELLINGTON

This recipe comes from the Wellington Club, one of London's oldest and most exclusive dining clubs, specializing in traditional English cuisine.

1 kg ($2^1/_4$ lb) beef fillet
5 tsp butter
250 g (9 oz) mushrooms
1 small onion, peeled
75 g (3 oz) smooth chicken liver pâté
2 tbsp fresh white breadcrumbs
1 sprig fresh thyme, chopped
salt and freshly ground black pepper
500 g (18 oz) chilled puff pastry
1 egg yolk to glaze

SHERRY SAUCE
5 tsp butter
4 tbsp flour
375 ml (13 fl oz) good beef stock
2 tsp tomato paste
4 tbsp medium cream sherry

1 Trim any fat from the fillet. Pre-heat the oven to 220 °C (425 °F/gas 7). Heat the butter in a roasting tin, and brown the fillet on all sides. Cook for 5 minutes if you like it rare, for 10 minutes for medium and for 15 minutes for a well-done fillet. Remove and cool.

2 Process the mushrooms and onion in a food processor, then add to the roasting tin and fry in the meat juices for about 5 minutes. Stir in the pâté, then cool. Stir in the breadcrumbs, thyme and seasoning.

3 Roll out the pastry on a lightly floured surface. Trim to a 40 x 45 cm (16 x 18 in) rectangle using a sharp knife. Spoon a little of the mushroom and onion mixture down the centre of the pastry. Place the fillet on top. Spoon the remaining mushroom and onion mixture over the top and sides of the fillet.

4 Brush the edges of the pastry with beaten egg yolk and fold pastry over like a parcel to enclose the fillet. Press the edges together to seal well. Trim excess pastry.

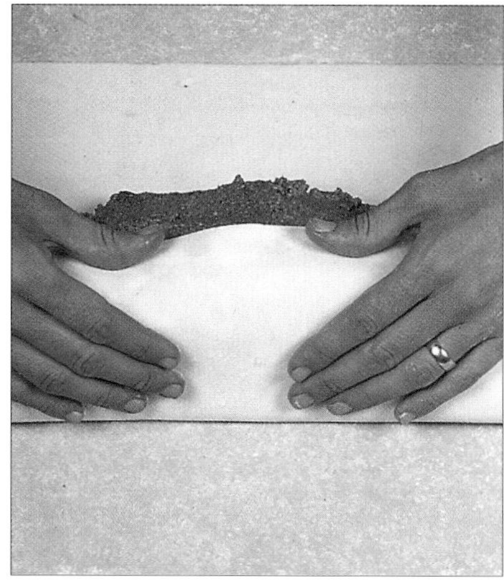

5 Place the Beef Wellington, joined side down, onto a lightly greased baking sheet. Brush the top with egg yolk.

6 Garnish with pastry trimmings: cut long strips with a pastry wheel and arrange on top. Make leaves by cutting pastry into triangles and marking with a sharp knife. Brush trimmings with egg yolk.

7 Bake at 200 °C (400 °F/gas 6) for 30–35 minutes. Cover with foil if it browns too quickly.

8 To make the sauce, melt butter in saucepan. Stir in flour and mix to a roux with a wooden spoon. Cook for 5 minutes until golden brown, to give the sauce a good colour. Gradually add the beef stock, tomato paste and sherry. Bring to the boil, reduce slightly, and season with salt and black pepper. Serve the sauce with Beef Wellington.
SERVES 6.

TOURNEDOS CHASSEUR

This is the perfect dish with which to splash out every now and then. Tournedos is the French name for a small thick steak cut from the centre of a fillet, and it is served on a fried bread croûte and topped with a sauce – my choice is rich mushroom sauce.

5 tsp oil
3 tbsp butter
4 slices of white bread, crusts removed
4 x 2–3 cm (¾ –1¼ in) thick tournedos
salt and freshly ground black pepper
3 tbsp chopped fresh parsley

CHASSEUR SAUCE
5 tsp butter
1 small onion, finely chopped
125 g (4½ oz) button mushrooms, sliced
120 ml (4 fl oz) dry white wine
50 ml (2 fl oz) tomato purée
150 ml (5 fl oz) beef stock
4 tbsp single cream
1 tbsp brandy

1 First make the sauce. Heat butter and sauté onion. Turn up the heat, add mushrooms and fry for 3–4 minutes, until soft.

2 Add the wine, tomato purée and beef stock, and cook until reduced by half. Add the cream and brandy and heat through. Set aside to serve with the tournedos.

3 To prepare the tournedos, pre-heat the oil and butter in a large saucepan and fry the bread on both sides until golden brown. Keep this fried bread croûte warm.

4 Turn up the heat, add more butter if necessary, and cook each tournedos over high heat for about 2 minutes per side (more if you prefer your meat well done). Season with salt and black pepper.

5 Arrange the meat on the toasted bread, pour the prepared sauce over the top, and garnish with a generous sprinkling of chopped parsley. Serve the tournedos immediately.
SERVES 4.

TIPS

◆ This dish is rich, so serve with a salad and plain vegetables.

◆ Grill the tournedos instead of frying, if preferred.

◆ Peel onions under cold, running water to prevent tears caused by their pungent smell.

STEAK AND KIDNEY PIE

750 g (1¾ lb) stewing beef, cubed
8 lamb's kidneys, cored and diced
1 x 340 ml (12 fl oz) can beer
60 g (2½ oz) plain flour
salt and freshly ground black pepper
2 tbsp butter
2 tbsp oil
2 onions, finely chopped
250 ml (8 fl oz) beef stock
300 g (11 oz) mushrooms, sliced
2 tbsp chopped fresh parsley
2 potatoes, peeled and cubed
350 g (12 oz) puff pastry
1 egg, beaten

1 Combine beef and kidneys in a bowl. Pour beer over the top, cover, and leave in the refrigerator for 2–4 hours.

2 Drain off the beer and reserve. Combine flour and seasoning, then toss beef and kidneys in the seasoned flour.

3 Pre-heat butter and oil. Fry onion until soft. Quickly brown beef and kidneys. Add reserved beer, stock, mushrooms and parsley.

4 Cover with a lid and simmer for 1½ hours on the hob. After 1 hour, add potatoes. Add more stock if necessary. Pour into an ovenproof pie dish.

5 Roll out the pastry and cut a lid to fit the dish. Wet the edges of the dish and cover with pastry. Press the edges down.

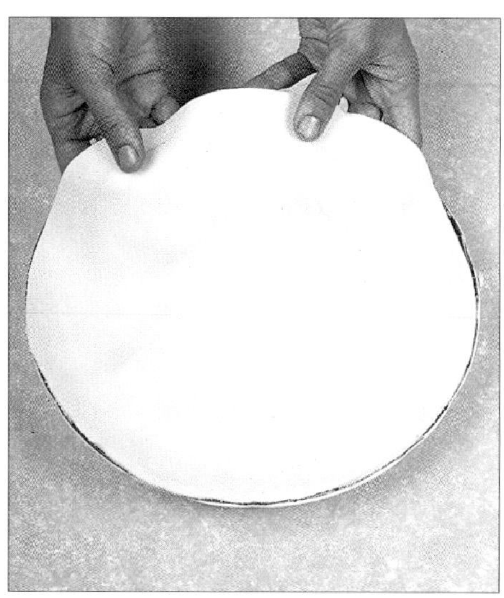

6 Brush the top with beaten egg. Bake in the oven at 200 °C (400 °F/gas 6) for 15–20 minutes, until golden brown.
SERVES 4–6.

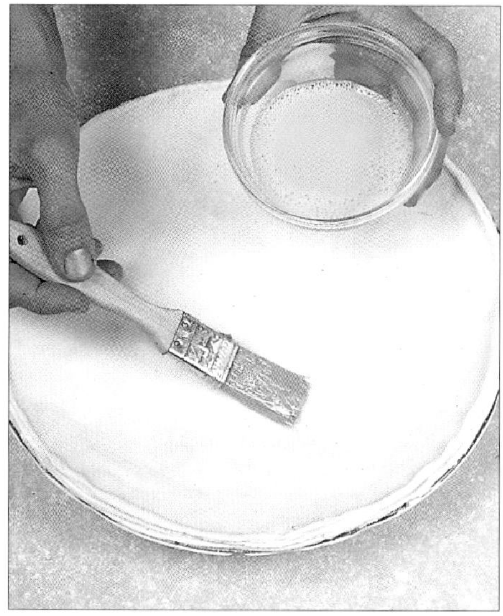

TIPS

- This dish freezes very well.
- Choose lamb's kidneys with a deep pink or beige colour, not red. Avoid any kidneys that smell of ammonia.
- If lamb's kidneys are unavailable, use ox kidneys.
- If you prefer not to marinate the meat in beer, simply omit step 1, combine the beef and kidneys, and toss in seasoned flour, as in step 2. Replace the beer with an equal quantity of extra beef stock in step 3.
- Puff pastry is made using equal quantities of flour and water and is therefore rather rich. It is ideal for pies, as it has a good, layered texture when cooked. The steam given off by the baking pie gives the pastry a good volume.

ROAST BEEF AND YORKSHIRE PUDDING

This English recipe includes Yorkshire pudding, which originally was intended to make the meat stretch: it was served first so that everyone could fill up on it before the meat was served!

1.3–1.5 kg (2¾–3¼ lb) beef joint (sirloin, rump or aitchbone)
2 cloves garlic, sliced into slivers
3 tbsp prepared French mustard
salt and freshly ground black pepper

YORKSHIRE PUDDING
125 g (4½ oz) plain flour
1 tsp salt
2 extra-large eggs
300 ml (10 fl oz) milk

1 Weigh the meat and calculate the cooking time: Rare – 20 minutes per 450 g (1 lb) plus an extra 20 minutes. Medium – 25 minutes per 450 g (1 lb) plus an extra 25 minutes. Well done – 30 minutes per 450 g (1 lb) plus an extra 30 minutes. Pre-heat the oven to 160 °C (325 °F/gas 3).

2 Make incisions all over the meat and insert slivers of garlic. Spread with prepared mustard and season with salt and black pepper.

3 Place the meat, fat-side up, on a trivet, and place the trivet on a rack directly above an approximately 18 cm (7 in) square dish to be used for the Yorkshire pudding. The juices from the meat provide the dripping for the Yorkshire pudding.*

4 Roast the meat, turning twice during cooking, and ending with the fat-side up.

5 To make the Yorkshire pudding, sift together flour and salt. Lightly beat together eggs and milk.

6 Make a well in the centre of the flour, and add the egg and milk mixture, beating until smooth. Cover and refrigerate for 30 minutes.

7 Approximately 40 minutes before the beef is cooked, remove the batter from the refrigerator and beat again. Increase the oven temperature to 200 °C (400 °F/gas 6), moving the meat higher up to the coolest part of the oven. Pour the Yorkshire pudding batter into the dish containing the hot dripping, and bake for 30–40 minutes.** Serve the Roast Beef and Yorkshire pudding with vegetables and gravy (to make gravy see box alongside).
SERVES 4–6.

TIPS

◆ To make delicious gravy, roast the beef in a roasting tin and use the dripping as the basis for the gravy: remove the meat from the roasting tin when cooked. Place the tin on the hob. Sprinkle in 1 tbsp flour and stir with a wooden spoon, allowing it to brown but not burn. Add 250 ml (8 fl oz) stock (the liquid from cooking the vegetables makes a good stock). Reduce and thicken. If desired, a wine glass of red or white wine or cream can be added for a richer gravy. Strain before serving.

* If using the dripping to make gravy, you will need to use a different method to cook the Yorkshire pudding: pre-heat 3 tbsp cooking oil in an 18 cm (7 in) square dish until piping hot, then pour the batter into the dish. Bake in the oven at 200 °C (400 °F/gas 6) with the roast beef for the final 30–40 minutes.

** Individual Yorkshire puddings also can be baked in muffin tins: pre-heat 2 tsp cooking oil in each muffin tin, then pour in the batter; cook for 15–20 minutes, until the Yorkshire puddings are well-risen and golden brown.

BRAISED LAMB SHANKS

Braised meat is cooked in a small amount of wine or stock, usually with vegetables, in a covered casserole. Lamb shanks are tasty and succulent, but order from your butcher in advance, as it is not a cut which is readily available.

6 lamb shanks
salt and freshly ground black pepper
2 tbsp oil
4 cloves garlic, crushed
4 spring onions, chopped
1 onion, chopped
1 carrot, diced
1 leek, diced
1 turnip, diced
1 tomato, peeled, seeded and chopped
1 tbsp tomato paste
120 ml (4 fl oz) white wine
2 sprigs thyme and rosemary
1 bay leaf
1 litre (1¾ pints) beef stock

1 Season lamb shanks with salt and pepper. Pre-heat oil in a flameproof casserole and brown the shanks on all sides, doing half at a time. Remove from the dish and set aside.

2 Add the garlic and all the vegetables to the dish and stir-fry for 3 minutes. Cover with a lid and allow the vegetables to sweat for 5 minutes.

3 Add tomato paste and stir through, then add wine to de-glaze the dish.

4 Return the shanks to the dish. Add thyme, rosemary, bay leaf and stock. Cover, and bake in the oven at 160 °C (325 °F/gas 3) for 2–3 hours.

5 When cooked, the meat will pull away from the bone. Remove the shanks from the dish, cover, and rest in the warming drawer.

6 Place the casserole on the hob, remove the lid and reduce the sauce until thickened.

7 The sauce can be served either in a gravy boat, or pour the sauce onto a serving platter and top with lamb shanks. Serve with boiled new potatoes, allowing 1 shank per person.
SERVES 6.

TIPS

- Lamb, is a tender, succulent meat. Insist of lamb and not mutton, which has a higher fat content and is less succulent.
- If desired, add a handful of pre-soaked dried fruit, e.g. apricots or peaches, to the dish in step 4.
- To peel tomatoes, cover with boiling water for 2 minutes, then hold under cold running water. Cut a small slit in the skin at the bottom of the tomato, and peel towards the top. If the skin does not peel easily, return to hot water and repeat. Cut out the stalk with a sharp knife.

OXTAIL STEW

Although oxtail falls into the category offal, it is excellent for stewing, braising and casseroling. It has a rich flavour and a thick, hearty texture when stewed, and is ideal on a cold winter's night.

1 oxtail, cut into portions
2 tbsp flour, seasoned with salt and pepper
3 tbsp oil
100 g (4 oz) streaky bacon
1 onion, chopped
2 large carrots, cut into rings
2 tbsp tomato paste
250 ml (8 fl oz) beef stock
250 ml (8 fl oz) red wine
bouquet garni (1 bay leaf, 4 peppercorns, 4 sprigs parsley and 4 cloves tied into a muslin bag)
strip of lemon peel
strip of orange peel
1 tbsp lemon juice
12 small pickling onions
chopped fresh parsley to garnish

1 Coat the oxtail in seasoned flour. Pre-heat oil in a large flameproof casserole. Brown the meat on all sides. Remove from the casserole and set aside.

2 Add bacon to casserole and fry until crisp. Break into small pieces and set aside. Add onion and carrots, and fry until onion is soft and golden brown.

3 Add tomato paste and return oxtail and bacon to casserole. Add stock, wine, bouquet garni, citrus peel and lemon juice. Simmer gently for 2–3 hours in the oven at 170 °C (325 °F/gas 3) or on the hob, stirring occasionally.

4 After $1\frac{1}{2}$ hours, add the pickling onions.

5 Before serving, remove the bouquet garni and the citrus peel. Garnish with the chopped parsley. Serve with creamy Mashed Potatoes (see p. 125) and lightly steamed green vegetables.
SERVES 4.

TIPS

- ◆ New potatoes may be added with the pickling onions.
- ◆ Buy ready jointed oxtail, as it is difficult to joint yourself.
- ◆ Remove all fat from the oxtail joints before cooking, or the stew may be rather fatty.
- ◆ Oxtail Stew always tastes best if made a day ahead and refrigerated overnight. Before re-heating, scrape off the thin layer of fat which will have formed on the top of the stew.
- ◆ Oxtail Stew freezes very well.

STICKY SPARE RIBS

Definitely a finger-smacking meal. Allow about 350–500 g (12–18 oz) fresh or smoked ribs per person.

approximately 2 kg (4½ lb) pork or lamb ribs
3 tbsp oil
grated rind of 1 orange
120 ml (4 fl oz) fresh orange juice
75 ml (2½ fl oz) soy sauce
3 tbsp tomato sauce
100 ml (3½ fl oz) fruit chutney
100 ml (3½ fl oz) clear honey
4 tbsp smooth apricot jam
1 tbsp prepared French mustard
2 tbsp Worcestershire sauce
1 tsp ground ginger
freshly ground black pepper

1 Cut the ribs into serving portions using a sharp knife. Place in a large dish, and set aside. Combine all the remaining ingredients in a saucepan and place over low heat, stirring until smooth and well mixed. Cool.

2 Spoon the cooled marinade over the spare ribs, cover, and leave to marinate in the refrigerator for at least 6 hours, or overnight.

3 Remove the ribs from the marinade, reserving marinade. Grill under a pre-heated grill or over hot coals, basting frequently with the marinade. Grill for 5 minutes per side if smoked, and 10 minutes per side if unsmoked.

4 The remaining marinade may be placed in a saucepan and simmered until reduced and thickened. Serve separately.

5 Arrange the spare ribs on pre-heated platters. Serve with baked potatoes or chips, as well as finger bowls and plenty of paper napkins.
SERVES 4.

TIPS

◆ Use any flavour juice in place of the orange juice.

◆ Many butchers cut spare rib from the breast section, but try to buy true pork spare rib cut from the triangular rib section at the bottom of the belly.

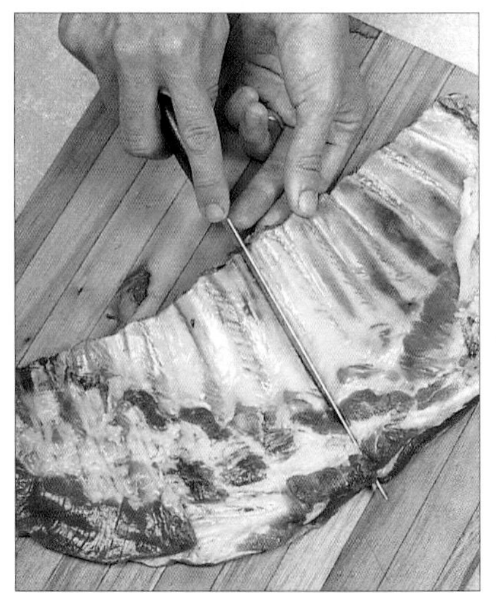

ROAST PORK WITH RED CHERRY SAUCE

Pork has a tendency to be a little dry. Choose a joint with a good covering of crackling and some fat – loin, rib on the bone, or leg are good for roasting.

1.5 kg (3¼ lb) pork joint
a little oil
salt

RED CHERRY SAUCE
175 g (6 oz) canned, stoned red cherries with juice
3 tbsp golden syrup
2 tbsp wine vinegar
salt and freshly ground black pepper
pinch of nutmeg
pinch of cinnamon
pinch of ground cloves
2 tsp cornflour slaked in 1 tbsp water

1 With a sharp knife, deeply score the rind of the pork.

2 For a crisp and golden brown crackling, rub the rind with oil and then salt.

3 Work out the cooking time: pork needs to be roasted for 25 minutes per 450 g (1 lb), plus an extra 30 minutes, at 160 °C (325 °F/gas 3), and is never served underdone. Therefore, a 1.5 kg (3¼ lb) roast will require a roasting time of 1¾ hours.

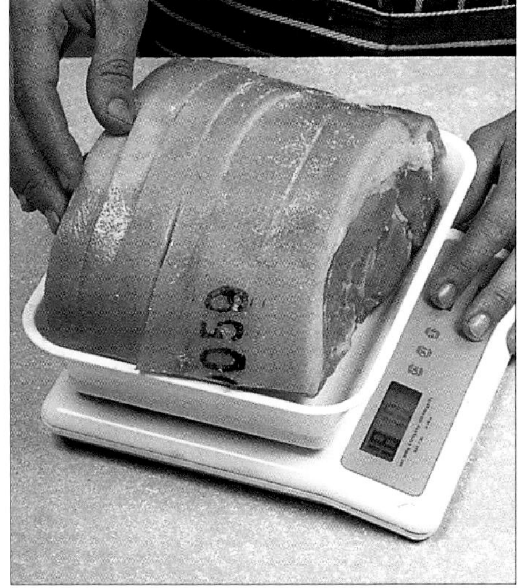

4 Roast with the rind facing up, and do not baste, as that will prevent the rind from becoming a perfectly crisp crackling. After cooking, cover and rest in the warming drawer for 15 minutes before carving.

5 Meanwhile, prepare the Red Cherry Sauce by combining all the ingredients except slaked cornflour in a saucepan. Bring to the boil and cook for 10 minutes, until the sauce is piping hot and heated through. Add cornflour and, stirring constantly, allow the sauce to thicken. If a smooth sauce is preferred, combine all ingredients in a food processor or blender and process until smooth. Re-heat the sauce, and serve piping hot with the Roast Pork.
SERVES 4–6.

TIPS

◆ To make traditional Apple Sauce instead of Red Cherry Sauce, core, peel and slice 4 Granny Smith apples, then place in a saucepan. Add 100 ml (3½ fl oz) water, 2 tsp lemon juice, 2–3 tbsp sugar and a knob of butter. Cook, covered, until very soft. Remove from the heat and mash with a fork, or process in a blender or food processor until smooth.

◆ Do not refrigerate pork for longer than 3–4 days.

COLD PRESSED TONGUE WITH OLIVES

I particularly enjoy the velvety texture of tongue, a meat that is often neglected. Ox, calf and lamb tongues are available, with ox tongue being the largest.

1 pickled tongue, approximately 1.5 kg (3¼ lb) in weight
water to cover
2 carrots, sliced
1 onion, quartered
3 sticks soup celery
fresh parsley
1 bay leaf
50 g (2 oz) stuffed olives
1 tsp gelatine
175 ml (6 fl oz) reserved stock

1 Wash brine off the tongue and place in a pressure cooker. Pour over enough cold water to just cover the tongue. Add carrots, onion, celery, parsley and bay leaf.

2 Cook in the pressure cooker on full steam for 75 minutes. If you don't have a pressure cooker, cook in a large saucepan on the hob for 3 hours, or until the tongue feels tender when pierced with a fork.

3 Reserve 175 ml (6 fl oz) stock. Allow the tongue to cool completely and then remove the tough outer skin. If the skin does not come away easily, the tongue requires further cooking.

4 Push the peeled tongue into a bowl or a cake tin with straight sides. The fit must be very tight to achieve a good pressing. Make incisions in the tongue with the point of a sharp knife. Insert olives into these holes.

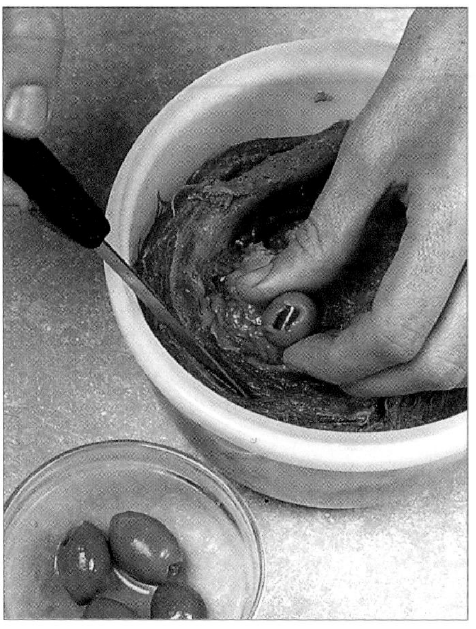

5 Sprinkle gelatine over reserved stock. Heat gently to dissolve the gelatine.

6 Pour the gelatine and stock mixture over the tongue. Press down firmly and refrigerate for at least 12 hours before serving. It is a good idea to keep it weighted down. Serve thinly sliced with a selection of salads.
SERVES 4–6.

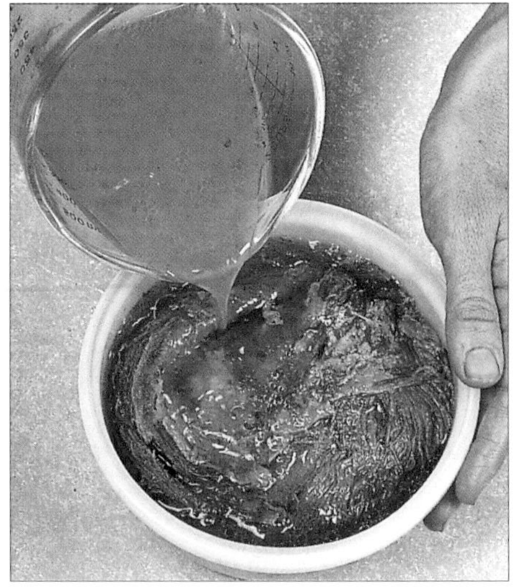

TIP

◆ Tongue can be successfully sliced with a bread slicer, and can be sliced very thinly if it is first well chilled.

VENISON STEW

Venison is a popular game meat with a flavour that varies from mild to pungent, depending on whether the animal has been hung. The advantage of this red meat is its surprisingly low cholesterol content.

250 g (9 oz) speck, cubed
2 kg ($4^1/_2$ lb) venison, cubed (any cut needing long, slow cooking may be used)
2 tbsp oil
2 onions, chopped
2 cloves garlic, crushed
2 carrots, sliced
2 sticks soup celery, sliced
1 tbsp flour
750 ml ($1^1/_4$ pints) meat stock or red wine
1 tbsp brown vinegar
5 cloves
1 tsp ground coriander
5 peppercorns
2 bay leaves

CARAWAY DUMPLINGS
125 g ($4^1/_2$ oz) plain flour
1 tsp baking powder
1 tbsp butter
1 large egg, beaten with 3 tbsp milk
2 tsp caraway seeds
salt and freshly ground black pepper

1 Pre-heat a large flameproof casserole and heat speck cubes, allowing the fat to run. Add venison and brown over high heat. Remove the venison and speck with a slotted spoon, and set aside.

2 Add oil to the casserole. Fry onions until soft and light gold. Add garlic, carrots and celery. Place the lid on the casserole, and allow to sweat for 3 minutes.

3 Return the venison and speck to the casserole, sprinkle flour over, and stir through. Add stock or wine, and vinegar. Add the remaining ingredients. Cover and simmer gently for 1–2 hours, depending on the age of the meat, until the venison is tender. Do not over-cook, as the venison may become very tough.

4 Prepare dumplings by sifting the flour and baking powder into a bowl. Rub in the butter with your fingertips until the mixture resembles breadcrumbs.

5 Add the egg and milk mixture. Fold in caraway seeds and seasoning.

6 Place spoonfuls of batter into the simmering casserole 15 minutes before serving. Cover, and cook for a further 15 minutes. SERVES 6.

TIP

◆ Top up the casserole with extra stock if necessary, as a good amount of moisture is needed in order to cook the dumplings, and remember to use dumpling batter immediately – do not allow it to stand.

TUNA LASAGNE

3 tbsp oil
1 large onion, finely chopped
1 clove garlic, crushed
250 g (9 oz) button mushrooms, sliced
2 x 185 g cans tuna, drained and flaked
1 x 400 g can good quality cream of tomato soup
100 ml ($3\frac{1}{2}$ fl oz) water
4 tbsp chopped fresh parsley
4 tbsp chopped fresh dill
$\frac{1}{2}$ tsp cayenne pepper

BECHAMEL SAUCE
1 small carrot, chopped
$\frac{1}{2}$ onion, chopped
1 stick celery, chopped
2 peppercorns
600 ml (1 pint) milk
4 tbsp butter
4 tbsp flour
1 tsp mustard powder
salt and freshly ground black pepper
8 spinach lasagne sheets (those that need no pre-cooking)
4 tbsp fresh breadcrumbs, white or brown
1 tbsp Parmesan cheese

1 Pre-heat the oil in a large saucepan, then fry the onion. Add the crushed garlic and fry for 1 minute. Add the mushrooms and fry until they have changed colour and have drawn moisture.

2 Add tuna, undiluted tomato soup and water. Add parsley, dill and cayenne pepper. Simmer for 5 minutes. Set aside.

3 To make Béchamel sauce, place carrot, onion, celery, peppercorns and milk in saucepan, bring to a gentle simmer, then set aside for 30 minutes.

4 Melt the butter and stir in the flour with a wooden spoon, to form a roux. Remove the saucepan from the heat.

5 Strain milk to remove the flavouring vegetables. Pour milk into butter and stir. Return to heat and continue stirring. Add mustard and seasoning. Allow to thicken, then set aside. Lightly grease a 28 x 18 cm (11 x 7 in) ovenproof dish. Pour half the fish mixture into the dish. Layer 4 lasagne sheets over the fish mixture, and then pour half the Béchamel sauce over the lasagne sheets. Repeat, ending with sauce.

6 Combine breadcrumbs and Parmesan cheese, and sprinkle over top. Bake at 180 °C (350 °F/gas 4) for 30 minutes, until golden brown and bubbling.
SERVES 6.

TIPS

- This dish freezes well.
- For a variation, replace tuna with mashed pilchards.
- Spinach lasagne can be replaced by plain lasagne sheets.
- Serve with a crisp, green salad and a crusty French loaf.

LUXURY MACARONI CHEESE

Macaroni cheese has gained the reputation of midweek stodge. This recipe, however, makes it a meal everyone will look forward to.

1 tbsp oil
250 g (9 oz) macaroni
1 large onion, finely chopped
5 tsp butter
2 large, ripe tomatoes
3 tbsp butter
3 tbsp flour
600 ml (1 pint) milk
1 tsp mustard powder
pinch of cayenne pepper
salt and freshly ground black pepper
200 g (7 oz) mature Cheddar cheese, grated
125 g (4½ oz) smoked ham, cubed, or bacon, fried and crumbled
2 tbsp fresh breadcrumbs
1 tbsp grated Parmesan cheese
paprika

1 Bring a large pan of salted water to the boil. Add oil to prevent pasta from sticking together. Cook macaroni for 10 minutes. Drain well and set aside.

2 Fry onion in 5 tsp butter until soft. Set aside. Pour boiling water over tomatoes and stand for 2–3 minutes. Remove and plunge into cold water, then peel off skin and cut into small cubes.

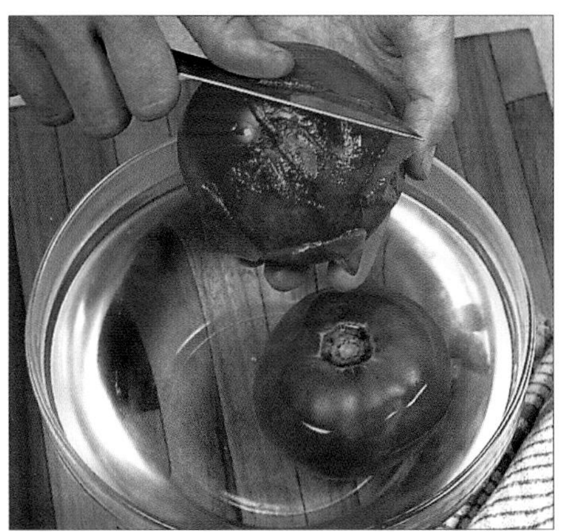

3 Prepare white sauce by melting 3 tbsp butter in pan. Add flour and stir to form a roux. Remove from heat and add milk. Return to heat and continue stirring until sauce thickens. Add mustard powder, cayenne pepper, seasoning and Cheddar cheese, and stir through until melted.

4 Combine sauce and macaroni. Layer ingredients in greased ovenproof dish – first macaroni, then onion, tomato and cubed ham or bacon.

5 Repeat the layers, ending with the macaroni.

6 Combine breadcrumbs and Parmesan cheese and sprinkle over the macaroni. Sprinkle the top with paprika. Bake at 180 °C (350 °F/gas 4) for 30 minutes, until the top is golden brown. Serve piping hot with a green salad.
SERVES 4–6.

TIPS

◆ Macaroni cheese freezes well.

◆ If preferred, ham and bacon can be omitted.

◆ White sauce can be made richer with the addition of approximately 120 ml (4 fl oz) cream or 2 eggs lightly beaten and added to the sauce at the end of step 3.

◆ Smoked Viennas or any other smoky sausage can replace the bacon or ham.

◆ Do not try and make this dish without mature Cheddar cheese. Ordinary Cheddar does not have a strong enough flavour.

PASTA WITH MUSHROOMS, PEAS AND HAM

This dish is good with any pasta shape, but is best with the long varieties, like spaghetti, fettuccine or tagliatelle.

2 tsp salt
1 tbsp oil
500 g (18 oz) pasta of your choice
3 tbsp butter
1 onion, finely chopped
250 g (9 oz) mushrooms, sliced
125 g ($4^1/_2$ oz) smoked ham, cut in one piece, then cut into strips
125 g ($4^1/_2$ oz) fresh shelled peas, or defrosted frozen peas
250 ml (8 fl oz) single cream
pinch of dried tarragon, or 1 tbsp chopped fresh tarragon
salt and freshly ground black pepper
50 g (2 oz) Parmesan cheese, grated

1 To cook pasta, bring a large pan of water to the boil, and add salt and cooking oil. (The oil prevents the pasta from sticking together.) Add the pasta to the boiling water and remove the lid from the pan. Depending on its thickness, most pasta will cook in 10–12 minutes.

2 While pasta is cooking, prepare sauce. Melt butter and fry onion until soft and golden, then add mushrooms and cook until mushroom liquid has evaporated, stirring from time to time.

3 Add ham and peas, and stir through. Add cream and tarragon, and season with salt and pepper. Heat through, but do not boil.

4 Drain the pasta, retaining 1 tbsp cooking liquid. Stir it through the pasta.

5 Spoon the hot cream sauce over the pasta and stir through. Serve immediately on piping hot plates, generously sprinkled with Parmesan cheese. Serve with a green salad.
SERVES 4.

TIPS

◆ To make a vegetarian meal, leave out the ham.

◆ For a variation, replace the ham with smoked sausage slices.

◆ Vegetables like courgettes, patty pan squash and red or green peppers can replace the peas, or add them as an extra.

◆ For a lower fat content, replace the cream with 250 ml (8 fl oz) chicken or vegetable stock. Check seasoning.

◆ Use any of the wide variety of commercially available pasta shapes for something different.

VEGETABLE LASAGNE

Omit the bacon for a delicious, meatless dish.

125 g (4½ oz) streaky bacon
2 onions, chopped
2 tbsp oil
2 cloves garlic, crushed
1 large carrot, grated
1 medium cabbage, chopped
1 x 400 g can whole peeled tomatoes, including juice
½ tsp grated nutmeg
1 tsp dried oregano
salt and freshly ground black pepper
approximately 12 sheets lasagne pasta (those that need no pre-cooking)

CHEESE SAUCE
3 tbsp butter
3 tbsp flour
600 ml (1 pint) milk
salt and freshly ground black pepper
1 tsp mustard powder
200 g (7 oz) Cheddar cheese, grated

1 Fry bacon until crisp, remove from the pan, and break into bite-sized pieces. Set aside.

2 Add onions and oil to the bacon fat and fry until soft.

3 Add garlic, carrot and cabbage. Stirring the mixture, fry over medium heat for 3 minutes.

4 Slice tomatoes and add with juice to cabbage mixture. Add nutmeg, bacon pieces, oregano and seasoning. Simmer over medium heat for 10 minutes. The mixture should not become too dry.

5 To make the cheese sauce, melt butter, add flour and mix to form a roux.

6 Remove from heat and add milk. Return to heat, and stir constantly until mixture thickens. Add salt, pepper, mustard and three-quarters of the grated cheese.

7 Pour half cabbage mixture into a large ovenproof dish, and cover with half the lasagne sheets, then half the cheese sauce. Repeat, ending with cheese sauce.

8 Sprinkle the remaining cheese over the top. Bake at 180 °C (350 °F/gas 4) for 30 minutes, until golden brown and bubbling. Serve with a salad.
SERVES 4–6.

TIPS

- To make meat lasagne, replace cabbage with 500 g (18 oz) beef mince, and proceed as above.
- Replace the cabbage with sliced or grated courgettes if liked.
- The flavour improves with standing, so make it the day before, cover, and refrigerate.
- 1 kg (2¼ lb) peeled, fresh red tomatoes can replace the canned variety.
- Replace 120 ml (4 fl oz) milk with cream, for a richer sauce.

SPAGHETTI BOLOGNESE

This meat sauce originated in the Italian city of Bologna.

2 tbsp olive oil
2 tbsp butter
1 large onion, chopped
4 sticks soup celery, sliced
1 carrot, peeled and grated
500 g (18 oz) lean beef mince
1 x 400 g can peeled tomatoes, sliced and juice reserved
120 ml (4 fl oz) white or red wine
250 ml (8 fl oz) water
2 tbsp tomato paste
1 tsp sugar
1 bay leaf
salt and freshly ground black pepper
1 tsp dried oregano, or 1 tbsp chopped fresh oregano
500 g (18 oz) spaghetti

1 Heat olive oil and butter, add onion and fry until soft, then add celery and carrot. Stir-fry for a few minutes.

2 Turn up heat, add mince, and brown, stirring to break up the mince lumps.

3 Add tomatoes with juice, wine, water, tomato paste, sugar, bay leaf, salt and pepper and oregano.

4 Cover and simmer very gently for 1 hour. Remove from heat and discard bay leaf.

5 Just before serving, bring a large pan of water to the boil. Add 1 tbsp oil and 1 tsp salt to water, then add spaghetti, and boil for 12 minutes. Drain, and serve with meat sauce: either serve individually on very hot plates, or serve the spaghetti and the sauce separately in large serving bowls, accompanied by a salad.
SERVES 4–6.

TIPS

◆ Some rashers of streaky bacon fried with the onion enhance the flavour of the sauce.

◆ This Bolognese Sauce freezes very well.

◆ It is a popular trend nowadays to make homemade pasta, and it really is quite simple: sift 400 g (14 oz) white bread flour into a heap on a surface. Make a hollow in the centre and break 3 eggs into the hollow. Add approximately 1–2 tbsp water. Using a fork in a circular motion, work in the eggs. Knead by hand until the dough is smooth. Shape into a ball, and rest, covered, for 30 minutes. Then knead quickly and divide the dough in half, keeping one half covered while you work on the other. Roll the dough out thinly and evenly on a floured surface. Cut into the desired shapes. Dry the pasta for at least 1 hour before using. Cook in boiling, salted water, and remember that homemade pasta cooks quickly, taking 4–6 minutes.

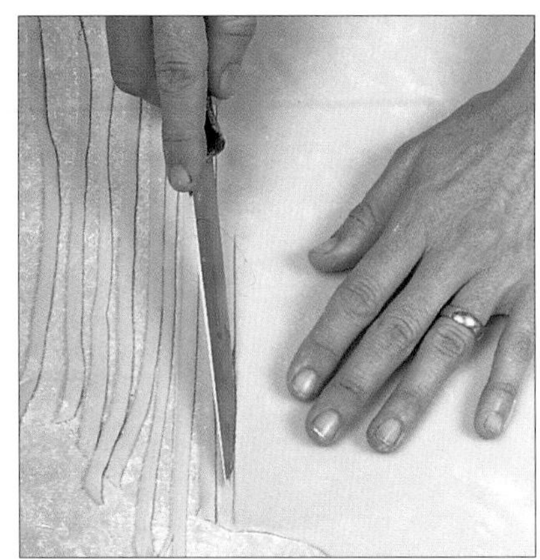

◆ To store celery, trim the sticks and place them in a jar of iced water in the refrigerator.

MUSSEL FETTUCCINE

A superb, velvety cream sauce that is perfect with fettuccine or tagliatelle. I like the mussels in their shells, but if preferred, the mussels can be served out of the shell.

1 x 900 g can black mussels
1 onion, sliced in rings
3 spring onions, finely chopped
1 clove garlic, crushed
3 tbsp butter
1 tbsp olive oil
2 tbsp flour
250 ml (8 fl oz) reserved mussel liquid
120 ml (4 fl oz) milk
120 ml (4 fl oz) dry white wine
120 ml (4 fl oz) single cream
1 tbsp chopped fresh dill
2 tbsp chopped fresh parsley
salt and freshly ground black pepper
approximately 400 g (14 oz) fettuccine or tagliatelle
chopped fresh parsley or dill to serve

1 Drain mussels through a fine sieve to remove all grit from liquid. Discard any closed mussels, and reserve liquid for the stock.

2 Fry onion, spring onions and garlic in butter and olive oil. Thicken with flour and remove from heat.

3 Stir in the mussel liquid, milk and wine. Return to the heat, and stir until thick.

4 Add cream, herbs, seasoning and mussels to sauce, and heat through without boiling. It is important to heat well, as mussels cool very quickly. Add more reserved mussel liquid if a thinner sauce is required.

5 To cook pasta, bring a large pan of water to the boil. Add 1 tbsp oil and 1 tsp salt. Add pasta, and boil for 12 minutes. Drain well.

6 Pre-heat a large serving dish. Place pasta in dish and pour sauce over the top, then stir through gently without damaging mussels. Sprinkle with chopped parsley or dill, and serve immediately: serve individual portions for an elegant starter, or larger portions accompanied by a colourful salad for a main meal.
MAKES 4–6 MAIN SERVINGS.

TIP

◆ Fresh mussels can be used in place of canned mussels. Scrub shells in a bowl of cold water. Place in a large saucepan, steam for 5 minutes, and discard any mussels that do not open during cooking. Replace reserved mussel liquid with 250 ml (8 fl oz) weak fish or chicken stock, and proceed as above.

SEAFOOD PASTA

This dish is called Pasta di Mare in its native Italy, where each region has its own version. The most common ingredients are shrimps, mussels and calamari, all served in a tasty tomato sauce. It is delicious served piping hot over your favourite shaped pasta – fusilli (screws), conchiglie (shells), lumache (snails), linguini or spaghetti – and topped with Parmesan cheese.

2 tbsp olive oil
1 onion, finely chopped
6 spring onions, chopped
1 small to medium carrot, grated
2 cloves garlic, crushed
500 g (18 oz) seafood mix (e.g. mussels, calamari and shrimps)
1 x 400 g can Italian peeled tomatoes, chopped and juice reserved
1 tbsp tomato paste
250 ml (8 fl oz) dry white wine
salt and freshly ground black pepper
1–2 tsp caster sugar
pinch of cayenne pepper
bouquet garni (1 large sprig fresh parsley, 1 bay leaf and 1 sprig fresh thyme or rosemary, tied together with a long string)
500 g (18 oz) pasta of your choice
2 tbsp chopped fresh parsley
grated Parmesan cheese to serve

1 Pre-heat the oil in a heavy-based saucepan. Fry onion until soft and golden. Add spring onions, carrot and garlic, and fry until soft but not brown.

2 Add seafood mix and stir-fry for 2 minutes.

3 Add tomatoes and juice, tomato paste and wine.

4 Season with salt and pepper. Sprinkle in the sugar and cayenne pepper.

5 Add the bouquet garni to sauce, hanging the end of the string over the edge of the pan for easy removal. Simmer sauce gently for 30 minutes, then remove the bouquet garni.

6 Meanwhile, cook pasta in a pan of rapidly boiling, salted water for about 12 minutes (this will vary according to pasta used). Drain well.

7 Spoon hot sauce over pasta, garnish with chopped parsley, and serve immediately, topped with plenty of Parmesan cheese and accompanied by a salad. Small portions can be served as a starter.
SERVES 4.

TIPS

◆ Freshly chopped chilli, or a little dried chilli, may be added to the sauce if desired.

◆ This sauce freezes well.

◆ Using fresh chillies can be quite tricky. Follow these hints:
- For a very hot dish, break off the stalk, wash the chilli and add to the dish.
- For a milder chilli dish, remove the seeds. To do this break off stalk, and halve the chilli lengthwise with a small sharp knife. (Rubber gloves can be used.) Take care not to rub your eyes. Scrape out the seeds, slice the chilli into thin strips and add to dish. Wash your hands thoroughly.

◆ Green chillies are juicy and very tasty, and red chillies are hotter.

MASHED AND ROAST POTATOES

There certainly is an art to producing delicious Roast and Mashed Potatoes. These simple directions will allow everyone to get them right the first time round – the Mashed Potatoes are light and fluffy, and the Roast Potatoes are deliciously crisp.

MASHED POTATOES
6 potatoes, peeled
4 tbsp butter
175 ml (6 fl oz) warm milk
salt and white pepper

ROAST POTATOES
4–6 large potatoes, peeled
fresh sunflower oil for roasting
salt

MASHED POTATOES

1 Halve the potatoes lengthwise but do not cut smaller as they would then easily overcook and become watery. Place potatoes in a saucepan, cover with water and add 1 tsp salt.

2 Bring the potatoes to the boil in the salted water and cook until the potatoes are just tender, but not falling apart.

3 Drain well, then return to the heat for 2 minutes to remove any excess moisture. Remove from the heat and transfer the potatoes to a mixing bowl. Add butter and milk. Mix with an electric hand beater until you reach a smooth texture. Do not overbeat. Check seasoning, and add to taste.

4 Spoon into a serving dish and serve immediately. If not hot enough, place in a pre-heated oven at 160 °C (325 °F/gas 3) for 5–10 minutes. Do not allow the mashed potatoes to dry out.
SERVES 4–6.

ROAST POTATOES

1 Halve the potatoes lengthwise, then, if they are very big, halve again to get quarters. Bring salted water to the boil in a large saucepan. Add the potatoes and boil for 15 minutes to par-cook. Cool slightly.

2 Pour 3 cm ($1^1/_2$ in) oil into an ovenproof dish, and pre-heat in the oven at 200 °C (400 °F/gas 6) for 15 minutes.

3 Score the cooled potatoes with the tines of a fork. Sprinkle with salt, then place in the hot oil, reduce the oven temperature to 180 °C (350 °F/gas 4), and bake for 45–60 minutes, turning for even browning. When cooked and crispy, remove from the oven and drain on absorbent paper before serving.
SERVES 4–6.

TIP

◆ Choose potatoes that are firm and smooth, have no soft spots or green or black discoloration, and no sprouted eyes.

SPICY POTATOES

This delicious Indian dish is a great accompaniment to meat, and is especially good served at a barbecue. This is also an excellent way to jazz up leftover potatoes.

4 tbsp oil
2 tsp ground cinnamon
1 tbsp ground coriander
1 tsp cayenne pepper
1 tbsp whole caraway seeds
2 tsp sesame seeds
2 tbsp butter
2.5 cm (1 in) piece of fresh ginger, peeled and grated
2 cloves garlic, crushed
750 g (1¾ lb) potatoes, unpeeled and cooked, then cut into 2.5 cm (1 in) square cubes
pinch of salt
4 tbsp chopped fresh coriander

1 Pre-heat oil in a heavy-based saucepan. When hot, add spices and seeds. When seeds pop, reduce heat. (Cooking the spices brings out their aromatic flavour.)

2 Add the butter, ginger and garlic. Cook for 1 minute, stirring constantly to prevent burning (if garlic burns, it becomes very bitter).

3 Add potatoes to the pan, and heat through for 8–10 minutes on medium heat, stirring occasionally to prevent them from catching on the bottom of the saucepan.

4 Season with salt and sprinkle with coriander. Spoon into a serving dish and serve the hot potatoes immediately.
SERVES 4–6.

TIPS

◆ Potatoes may be peeled if preferred. If they are peeled, store them immersed in cold water for no longer than 1 hour.

◆ If you are using leftover potatoes, heat through for a shorter period – about 6 minutes.

◆ Ground ginger can be used to replace the fresh ginger if absolutely necessary, although it will not produce quite the same result – use 1½–2 tsp.

◆ It is the root of the ginger plant that is used for cooking, and whole fresh ginger should be smooth-skinned, and kept in a cool, dry place, or it will sprout and become tasteless.

◆ Fresh coriander has a strong and distinctive flavour. It is widely used throughout the world, and is called *cilantro* in Spain and Mexico, and *dhania* in India. It must be used when very fresh – to keep a bunch of coriander fresh for a few days, place the roots in a jug of fresh water on a windowsill.

◆ Sesame seeds contain protein and minerals, and have a high oil content. Toasting them lightly brings out their flavour. To toast, spread out on a baking sheet and toast in a slow oven until they are light brown. Be careful not to let them burn.

◆ All spices can be stored in a cool, dark place for up to 1 year, but remember that it is always best to buy small quantities as needed and to use them as soon as possible.

ASPARAGUS WITH LEMON BUTTER SAUCE

Fresh asparagus is a common sight in the greengrocer in spring and early summer. My favourite variety is green asparagus, as it is tastier and more tender than others. This Lemon Butter Sauce is particularly good with the asparagus, and is also delicious served with vegetable dishes and fish.

300 g (11 oz) fresh green asparagus
salted water

LEMON BUTTER SAUCE
4 tbsp white wine
2 tbsp cream
175 g (6 oz) butter, diced
4 tbsp lemon juice
1 tsp Tabasco sauce
pinch of salt
strips of lemon rind to garnish

1 Wash the asparagus and cut off the woody ends using a sharp knife. Bring a shallow pan of salted water to the boil.

2 Add asparagus to the boiling water and cook, uncovered, for 15–20 minutes, or until just tender – the length of cooking time depends on the thickness of the asparagus stalks.

3 While the asparagus is cooking, prepare the lemon butter sauce. Combine the wine and cream in a small saucepan, and boil until reduced by half.

4 Gradually add the butter, stirring constantly using a wooden spoon, then add the lemon juice, Tabasco and salt.

5 Whisk thoroughly with a wire whisk until frothy.

6 Remove asparagus from the pan with a slotted spoon, and arrange on a serving dish. Pour hot sauce over, garnish with lemon rind, and serve immediately.
SERVES 3.

TIPS

◆ Asparagus may be prepared quickly in a microwave: wash, place half the asparagus in a single layer in a microwave-proof dish, add 2 tbsp cold water, cover with cling film, and microwave on High for 5 minutes. Repeat with the remaining asparagus.

◆ Asparagus is also excellent served cold with mayonnaise.

◆ If asparagus is served as a separate course, it is traditionally eaten with the fingers.

◆ To store asparagus, trim the stalks and stand in a jar of cold water, or wrap in a damp cloth. Refrigerate for 1–2 days.

RATATOUILLE

Serve this delicious dish either hot or cold. The proportions of the vegetables used may be varied, but take care not to make the dish too moist by using too many watery vegetables.

1 medium aubergine, sliced and quartered
2 courgettes, sliced
salt
2 onions, sliced
2 juicy cloves garlic, crushed
2 tbsp butter, melted
3 tbsp olive oil
1 each green, red and yellow pepper, seeded and sliced
100 g (4 oz) button mushrooms
1 x 400 g can peeled tomatoes, drained and chopped
3 tbsp red wine
1 tbsp tomato paste
2 tsp sugar
salt and freshly ground black pepper
chopped fresh basil, oregano and parsley

1 Sprinkle the aubergine and courgettes with salt, and stand for 30 minutes. Wash, then dry well with absorbent paper.

2 In a large flameproof casserole with a lid, fry onions and garlic in the butter and oil. Add peppers, mushrooms, tomatoes, aubergine and courgettes.

3 Add the wine, tomato paste, sugar, salt and a generous sprinkling of pepper.

4 Cover and simmer gently for 45 minutes. Add the fresh herbs and simmer for a further 30 minutes. Serve hot or cold as a vegetable course.
SERVES 4–6.

TIPS

◆ Serve cold Ratatouille with Yoghurt Sauce. To make the Yoghurt Sauce, combine 120 ml (4 fl oz) natural yoghurt, 5 tsp single cream, 1 clove crushed garlic, 2 tsp chopped fresh chives and 1 tsp fresh dill.

◆ Leftover Ratatouille makes an excellent filling for an omelette.

◆ Aubergines are a most versatile vegetable. Use them to make this simple and delicious 'Poor Man's Caviar'. Wrap 2 large aubergines in foil, and bake at 190 °C (375 °F/gas 5) for 1 hour, or until soft. Scoop out the flesh, add 3 cloves garlic, salt and black pepper to taste and 2 tbsp chopped fresh parsley, and purée in a food processor until smooth. Mix in 120 ml (4 fl oz) natural yoghurt if desired. Serve as a spread with bread or crisp savoury biscuits.

◆ Aubergines should be dégorged to remove excess moisture and bitter juices before cooking. To dégorge, slice, then sprinkle the flesh with salt and leave to stand for 30 minutes. Rinse thoroughly with cold water, and then dry well.

AUBERGINE AND TOMATO BAKE

Melanzana is the Italian word for aubergine or brinjal – a versatile vegetable so often neglected in cooking. Here they are used in a favourite dish often served as an antipasto in Italian restaurants. This perfect starter also makes a good light luncheon dish.

2 large or 3 medium aubergines
salt
olive oil
2 onions, finely chopped
3 tbsp cooking oil
2 cloves garlic, crushed
1 x 400 g can peeled tomatoes, sliced and juice reserved
1 tbsp tomato paste
1 tsp sugar
salt and freshly ground black pepper
1 tsp dried basil, or
1 tbsp chopped fresh basil
1 tsp dried oregano, or
1 tbsp chopped fresh oregano
200 g (7 oz) mozzarella cheese, sliced
3 tbsp grated Parmesan cheese

1 Wash and slice the aubergines, but don't peel. Sprinkle them with salt, and leave to stand for 20 minutes to draw out the vegetables' bitter juices.

2 Rinse the sliced aubergines well, and dry. Brush both sides of the slices with olive oil. Place on a baking sheet and grill under pre-heated grill. Once softened and lightly browned, turn, and brown on the other side. Take care as they burn easily.

3 Using a saucepan, fry the onions in the cooking oil until softening and golden brown. Add the garlic, tomatoes with juice, tomato paste, sugar, seasoning and herbs. Simmer for 10 minutes, until thickened.

4 Arrange half the aubergine slices in an ovenproof dish. Top with half the tomato mixture, then with half the mozzarella and half the Parmesan. Repeat layers, ending with the Parmesan.

5 Bake at 190 °C (375 °F/gas 5) for 30–40 minutes, until it is bubbling and the top is crisp.
SERVES 2–4.

TIPS

◆ Ricotta cheese can replace the mozzarella cheese.

◆ Top the Aubergine and Tomato Bake with fresh breadcrumbs instead of grated Parmesan cheese, if preferred.

◆ The sauce can be made using 1 kg ($2\frac{1}{4}$ lb) fresh tomatoes instead of canned tomatoes: skin and chop, and proceed as above.

◆ Prepare this dish up to the end of step 4 in advance, then cover and freeze or refrigerate for a couple of days. Proceed with step 5 just before eating.

SPINACH AND BUTTERNUT GNOCCHI

Gnocchi is an Italian dumpling, served as an attractive starter or as a light meal. I particularly love the tasty combination of these two flavours.

SPINACH GNOCCHI
500 g (18 oz) fresh spinach
100 g (4 oz) Ricotta cheese
5 tsp grated Parmesan cheese
1 extra-large egg
salt and freshly ground black pepper
pinch of nutmeg
flour
melted butter and grated Parmesan cheese to serve

BUTTERNUT SQUASH GNOCCHI
2 medium butternut squash
1 extra-large egg
flour
salt and white pepper
nutmeg
melted butter and grated Parmesan cheese to serve

1 To make the Spinach Gnocchi, tear the spinach leaves from the stalks and discard the stalks. Bring 120 ml (4 fl oz) salted water to the boil, add spinach, and cook for 3 minutes. Drain well, and chop with a knife or in a food processor.

2 Add Ricotta and Parmesan cheese. Beat the egg, add seasoning and nutmeg, and add to the spinach mixture. Add enough flour to obtain a dough that is neither too moist nor too dry.

3 On a floured surface, divide the dough into equal pieces and roll them into sausage shapes approximately 1–2 cm (½–¾ in) thick. Then cut into 2 cm (¾ in) long pieces. Place the gnocchi on the concave part of a fork and press against the prongs with a finger. Place on a baking sheet.

4 Bring a large pan of salted water to the boil. Drop the gnocchi into the water with a slotted spoon, and cook for about 1–2 minutes – they will float to the surface. Meanwhile, place some melted butter in the bottom of a heated dish, and transfer the cooked spinach gnocchi to the heated dish. Sprinkle with grated Parmesan cheese and serve immediately.

5 To make Butternut Squash Gnocchi, peel the butternut squash and cook in water until soft. Drain and mash.

6 Lightly beat the egg and add to the butternut squash with enough flour to form a tacky mixture. Season with salt, pepper and nutmeg.

7 Proceed with steps 3 and 4, as for Spinach Gnocchi.
SERVES 8 AS A STARTER.

TIPS

- Frozen spinach, defrosted, drained well and chopped, can be used instead of fresh.
- Gnocchi is excellent served with homemade tomato sauce.

VEGETABLE STRUDEL

A delicious surprise: layers of fresh vegetables wrapped up in a delicate parcel of filo pastry.

400 g (14 oz) broccoli florets
200 g (7 oz) fresh green beans, topped and tailed
150 g (5 oz) mangetout, or sugar snap peas
½ bunch of spring onions
4 courgettes, cut lengthwise
200 g (7 oz) carrots, peeled, and grated or julienned
8–10 sheets of filo pastry
200 g (7 oz) butter, melted
salt and freshly ground black pepper

1 Bring a large pan of water to the boil and season with 2 tsp salt. Then blanch the vegetables: place them in the boiling water for 1 minute, then remove and plunge them into cold water. Set aside.

2 To prepare the pastry, take 1 sheet of filo pastry and brush with the melted butter. Layer the next sheet on top of the first, and brush with melted butter. Repeat, until all the pastry has been used.

3 To make the strudel, layer the blanched broccoli florets to form a tightly packed pattern in the centre of the pastry, leaving 8 cm (3 in) pastry uncovered at each end. Season the layer, then repeat with the remaining vegetables, until they are all layered one on top of the other.

4 Fold the ends of the pastry over the vegetables, and roll up firmly, painting the pastry with melted butter as you roll.

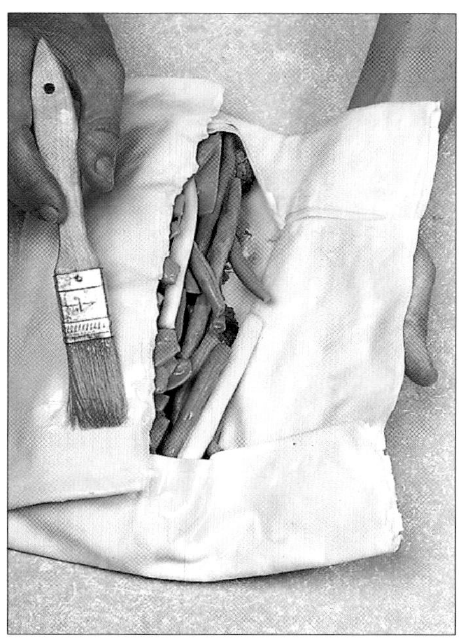

5 Place the strudel on a baking sheet and bake at 180 °C (350 °F/gas 4) for approximately 45 minutes, or until golden brown. Remove from the oven and stand for 5 minutes before slicing with a very sharp knife.
SERVES 6 AS A SIDE DISH.

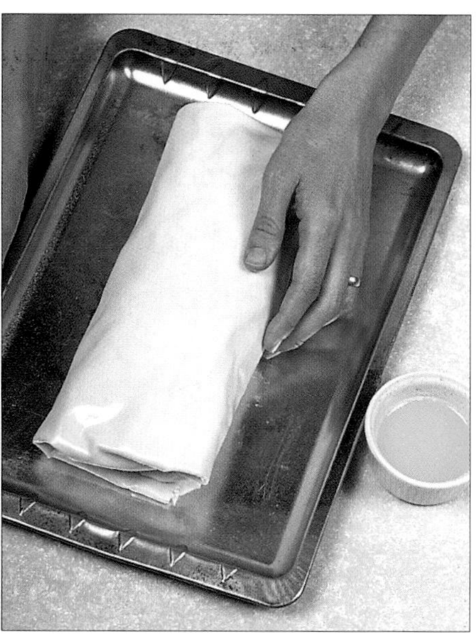

TIPS

- It is important to pack the vegetables closely together and roll up the filo pastry layers tightly, for a good overall effect.
- Slicing this strudel neatly can be tricky – use an electric carving knife for the best results.
- If vegetables are unavailable, vary according to seasonal availablity, or replace them with frozen vegetables.
- If preferred, brush the filo pastry with sunflower or olive oil instead of melted butter.
- Make ahead to end of step 4, cover well, and refrigerate for up to 4 hours before baking.

COURGETTE PIE

Courgettes are also known as baby marrows or zucchini. This vegetarian pie can be baked as individual tartlets, and makes a tasty savoury snack.

2 tbsp butter
1 onion, finely chopped
2 cloves garlic, crushed
1 large carrot, finely grated
400 g (14 oz) courgettes, finely grated
2 tbsp plain flour
1 tsp mustard powder
3 extra-large eggs, lightly beaten
salt and freshly ground black pepper
½ tsp ground nutmeg
2 tbsp finely chopped fresh parsley
100 g (4 oz) mature Cheddar cheese, grated
2 tbsp grated Parmesan cheese

1 Melt butter in a saucepan, add onion and sauté until soft and golden. Add garlic and sauté for 1 minute.

2 Add carrot and courgettes to the onion and garlic mixture, and sauté for 3 minutes.

3 Add flour and mustard powder to the eggs, and mix in a large bowl with a balloon whisk until lump-free. Add seasoning, nutmeg and parsley.

4 Fold the onion, carrot and courgette mixture into the egg mixture, and mix thoroughly. Fold in the grated Cheddar and Parmesan cheese.

5 Pour into a greased 18 x 28 cm (7 x 11 in) or 20 cm (8 in) round ovenproof dish. Bake at 180 °C (350 °F/gas 4) for about 20–30 minutes, until set. Or, to make tartlets, spoon mixture into muffin tins until three-quarters full. Bake at 180 °C (350 °F/gas 4) for 15–20 minutes. Serve warm. SERVES 6.

TIPS

◆ The Courgette Pie and tartlets freeze well: cover and store in the freezer for up to 3 months.

◆ Store eggs in a very cool place or in the refrigerator. Bring to room temperature before using.

SPINACH SALAD WITH CROUTONS

Tasty croûtons add a delicious crunch!

6 rashers rindless streaky bacon
200 g (7 oz) spinach
1 small butterhead lettuce
2 tsp caster sugar
1 small onion, finely sliced
1 red pepper, sliced
2 avocados, stoned, peeled and sliced, and dipped in a little lemon juice

CROUTONS
sunflower oil
2 x 2 cm (3/4 in) thick slices of stale white bread, crusts removed and cubed

DRESSING
25 g (1 oz) feta or Rosetta cheese, or other strong-flavoured cheese (optional)
2 cloves garlic, crushed
3 tbsp olive oil
3 tbsp vinegar
1 tbsp water
1 tsp sugar
1 tsp mustard powder
salt and freshly ground black pepper

1 Fry bacon in a pan. Cool and drain on absorbent paper, then break into bite-sized pieces and set aside. Reserve bacon fat for frying croûtons.

2 Wash spinach and lettuce leaves. Tear the spinach from stalks (unless using baby spinach), and tear the leaves into bite-sized pieces. Combine the spinach and lettuce in a salad bowl.

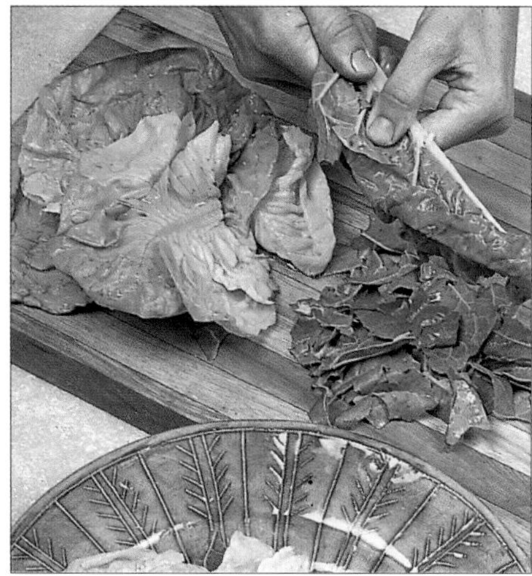

3 Sprinkle caster sugar, bacon pieces, onion, red pepper and avocado over the green leaves.

4 To make croûtons, add oil to bacon fat in the pan, to reach a depth of 1 cm (1/2 in). Fry bread cubes on all sides until crisp and golden brown.

5 Drain on absorbent paper and add to the salad.

6 To make dressing, crumble cheese, if using, into a small bowl. Add garlic, oil, vinegar and water. Mix, then add sugar and mustard powder. Season with salt and pepper. Serve dressing separately, or pour over salad just before serving and toss.
SERVES 4–6.

TIPS

◆ Cocktail tomatoes are an attractive optional extra.

◆ Garlic is best chopped rather than minced in a garlic press: set the flat side of a chef's knife on top of the unpeeled clove of garlic, and strike with your fist. Peel off the papery skin and chop the garlic with the knife, using small movements and moving the knife backwards and forwards.

◆ Spinach is a popular leaf vegetable rich in vitamins and minerals, especially iron. When it is cooked, spinach loses most of its iron traces, so it is more nutritious when eaten raw, as in this salad.

SALAD WITH BLUE CHEESE DRESSING

The combination of pecan nuts and blue cheese gives this salad a tasty tang.

1 head of lettuce – butterhead, iceberg, or a mixture of leaves
1 apple, sliced and dipped in a little lemon juice to prevent discoloration
1 green, red or yellow pepper, seeded and sliced
½ cucumber, sliced
1 stick table celery, sliced
1 avocado, cubed and dipped in a little lemon juice to prevent discoloration

DRESSING
50 g (2 oz) blue cheese
50 g (2 oz) pecan nuts
175 ml (6 fl oz) natural yoghurt
3 tbsp sour cream or buttermilk
3 tbsp olive or sunflower oil
2 tsp lemon juice
1 clove garlic, crushed
freshly ground black pepper
2 tsp sugar
1 tbsp freshly chopped parsley
extra blue cheese for topping (optional)

1 To prepare the salad, wash the lettuce and place in a large salad bowl.

2 Toss in the apple slices, pepper, cucumber, celery and cubed avocado.

3 Prepare the dressing by combining blue cheese and nuts in a food processor fitted with a metal blade. Pulse until combined but still chunky.

4 Add yoghurt, sour cream or buttermilk, and olive or sunflower oil through the feed tube, and combine.

5 Add lemon juice, garlic, black pepper, sugar and parsley through the feed tube. Combine.

6 The blue cheese dressing may be served separately, or it may be tossed through the salad just before serving.

7 Sprinkle grated blue cheese over the salad, if desired. Serve immediately.
SERVES 4–6.

TIPS

◆ Add cocktail tomatoes for an attractive optional extra.

◆ Blue cheese is a soft, ripened cheese, with a strong flavour. The blue veins are caused by a specially introduced mould. Like Roquefort, the original French blue cheese, it is creamy and firm, but with a crumbly texture owing to the blue-green mould.

◆ The salad dressing tastes better if made the day before. Store in the refrigerator.

◆ Use extra-virgin, cold-pressed olive oil for the best results.

◆ Vary the salad ingredients to suit seasonal availability.

GRILLED PEPPER SALAD

A Mediterranean favourite. The combination of green, red and yellow peppers makes a colourful feast, and is also a delicious addition to an antipasto platter.

4 large green, red or yellow peppers
3 cloves garlic, crushed
3 tbsp olive oil
salt to taste
freshly ground black pepper

1 Pre-heat grill, place whole peppers on a baking sheet and grill until skins start to blister and blacken. Watch carefully, and turn peppers to blacken all over. Alternatively, the peppers can be blackened by placing them on a baking sheet in a pre-heated oven at 200 °C (400 °F/gas 6) for 20–30 minutes. This method can make the peppers less crisp, but is more manageable.

2 Cool the peppers until they can be handled. Peel off the outer skin, or loosen the skins by placing the hot peppers in an ovenproof cooking bag and first allowing them to sweat, then peel.

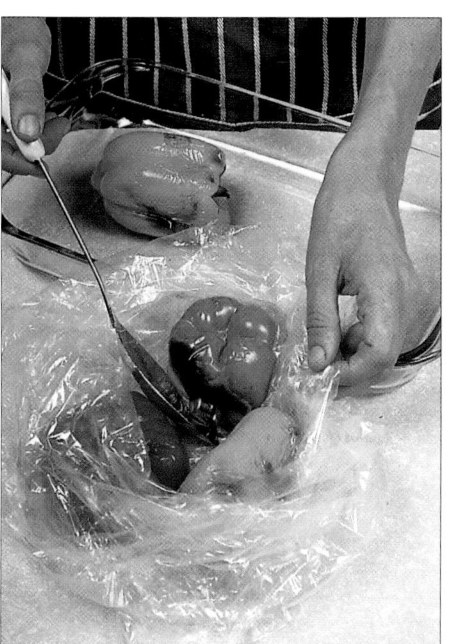

3 Seed the peppers and slice into thin strips. Place in a serving bowl.

4 Combine the garlic, olive oil, salt and a generous sprinkling of black pepper. Pour over peppers, then cover and cool before serving. This salad tastes even better on the second day.
SERVES 4.

TIPS

◆ 1–2 tbsp fresh lemon juice can be added with the rest of the ingredients in step 4 for extra flavour and tang.

◆ This recipe can be doubled.

◆ It keeps well for a couple of days – place in a sterilized glass jar, close tightly and refrigerate.

◆ Sweet peppers are relatives of the hot chilli pepper and are available in a rainbow of colours – green, red, yellow, orange and purple.

◆ Peppers are delicious stuffed and baked. Cut off the stalks, remove the seeds and ribs, and fill with a rice-based stuffing. Bake at 190 °C (375 °F/gas 5) for 20–30 minutes.

◆ Peppers contain no cholesterol or fat, and plenty of vitamin C.

◆ Thyme, oregano and capers complement sweet peppers well.

◆ Buy smooth, firm peppers, and avoid those that are soft or wrinkled, or have any dark spots.

MEXICAN AVOCADO LAYER

This avocado layer is an interesting variation on guacamole – that delicious Mexican treat. It makes an excellent starter, and is also good served with drinks or as an accompaniment to a buffet spread. Serve with crusty French or Italian bread or Melba toast.

1 large, or 2 medium ripe avocados
1 tbsp fresh lemon juice
salt and freshly ground black pepper
2 x 400 g cans tomato and onion mix
2 fresh chillies, seeded and sliced, or 1–2 tsp chilli powder
1 tsp sugar
1 bunch spring onions, finely chopped
250 ml (8 fl oz) cultured sour cream
100 g (4 oz) mature Cheddar cheese, grated
1 tsp paprika

1 Peel avocado and place in a food processor fitted with a metal blade. Add lemon juice and salt and pepper. Process until still a little chunky. (This can also be done with a potato masher.) Spread into the base of an oval 28 x 18 cm (11 x 7 in) serving dish.

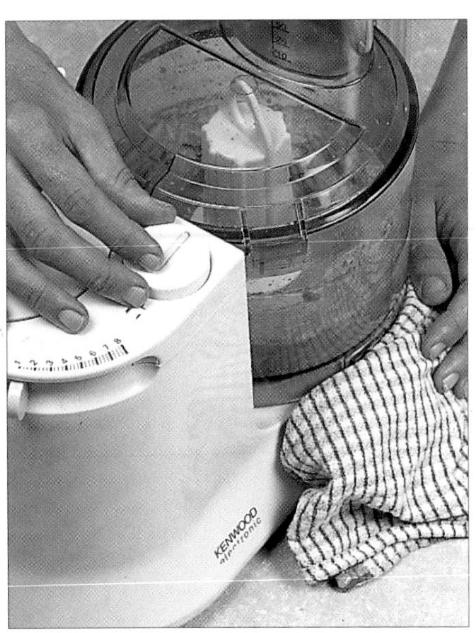

2 Pour tomato and onion mix into a colander and drain for 20 minutes. Pour into a mixing bowl and stir in chilli or chilli powder, sugar and finely chopped spring onions.

3 Spoon tomato mixture over avocado layer.

4 Spread sour cream over tomato mixture. Top with Cheddar cheese, and finally sprinkle with paprika.
SERVES 6.

TIPS

◆ This dish may be made a day ahead. Keep well covered in the refrigerator, and remove 1 hour before serving.

◆ Avocados are the fruit of the sub-tropical avocado tree, and are a food high in nutritional value: they are rich in natural oils, vitamins (especially vitamin C) and minerals.

◆ Slightly acidic citrus flavours complement the creamy flavour and cut the richness of avocados.

◆ The best way to ripen avocados is to wrap them in newspaper and store in a dark cupboard for 2–3 days.

◆ Avocado pulp freezes very well: remove the pulp from the avocado and place in a small bowl, mash, and add 1 tbsp lemon juice per avocado. Place in a glass jar with a screw-top lid. Three-quarters fill the glass jar, screw down the lid and freeze. Keep frozen for up to 1 year.

◆ To prevent a dish using avocado pulp from discolouring, store with the stone in the dish, and remove just before serving.

◆ If cultured sour cream is unavailable, add 1 tbsp lemon juice or white vinegar to fresh cream. Stir through and stand for 15 minutes before using.

◆ Always use mature Cheddar cheese when cooking as it has the most flavour.

◆ Use green chillies for a slightly milder flavour, or red chillies for a stronger flavour.

100
G

TABBOULEH SALAD

Grains are becoming increasingly popular in the culinary world, both because of their interesting flavour and in the name of healthy eating. Tabbouleh Salad is a Lebanese dish using bulgur (also known as cracked wheat) – an ingredient that has been used in Middle Eastern foods for thousands of years.

250 g (9 oz) bulgur
water to cover
2 medium, ripe tomatoes
1 bunch of spring onions, or 1 medium onion, finely chopped
1/4 cucumber, unpeeled and cubed
1 green or red pepper, seeded and finely chopped
25 g (1 oz) finely chopped fresh parsley
15 g (1/2 oz) chopped fresh mint

DRESSING
120 ml (4 fl oz) olive oil
120 ml (4 fl oz) fresh lemon juice
2 cloves garlic, crushed
1 tsp sugar
salt and freshly ground black pepper

1 Cover bulgur with water and soak for 30 minutes. (Bulgur is pre-cooked, and only needs to be soaked for use in salads.) Drain, and squeeze out in a clean cloth to remove all excess moisture.

2 To skin tomatoes, pour boiling water over them and stand for 2 minutes. Peel off skin, cut out stalk with a sharp knife, then cut in half and cube.

3 Combine tomatoes with spring onions, cucumber, pepper, parsley and mint. Mix in bulgur.

4 To make dressing, combine all ingredients well, and then pour dressing over bulgur. Cover and refrigerate for at least 2 hours, then stir through and serve.
SERVES 4–6.

TIPS

◆ Fresh mint is an essential part of this salad: do not replace it with dried mint – the taste will not be the same.

◆ This salad can be made in advance and refrigerated for 24 hours before serving.

◆ Bulgur is a useful grain that can replace rice as a side dish to a main course meal. To prepare bulgur, bring 1 litre (1 3/4 pints) water seasoned with 2 tsp salt to the boil, stir in 200 g (7 oz) bulgur, reduce the heat and simmer gently, with the lid on. Stir occasionally. Simmer for 15 minutes, then drain if necessary, and serve.

◆ Grains can become infested with weevils if not stored correctly. Store tightly sealed in the refrigerator for up to 6 months, or in the freezer for up to 1 year. Use straight from the freezer without first defrosting.

◆ To crush garlic, first peel, then sprinkle garlic clove with 1 tsp salt and work to a paste with the flat side of a knife blade.

A GOOD POTATO SALAD

Traditional potato salad with mayonnaise is a tired combination, but this delicious potato salad is a spicy variation.

1 kg ($2\frac{1}{4}$ lb) potatoes (approximately 6–8 large potatoes), peeled and quartered

DRESSING
120 ml (4 fl oz) olive oil
4 tbsp vinegar
3 tbsp fresh lemon juice
2 cloves garlic, crushed
2 tsp spicy curry powder
$\frac{1}{2}$ tsp Chinese Five-Spice powder*
3 tbsp finely chopped fresh coriander**
1 tsp sugar
1 tsp mustard powder
salt and freshly ground black pepper

1 Place potatoes in a pan, cover with water and add 1 tsp salt. Bring to the boil and allow the potatoes to soften, but do not overcook or they will become mushy and will fall apart.

2 Drain off water and cool potatoes just until they can be handled. Place in a serving dish or bowl.

3 While potatoes are cooking, prepare dressing. Whisk together oil, vinegar, lemon juice, garlic, curry powder and Chinese Five-Spice powder. Add fresh coriander, sugar, mustard powder and seasoning, and combine.

4 Pour the dressing over the potatoes – the secret of this recipe is to do this while the potatoes are still warm, allowing them to soak up the delicious dressing. Cover and stand for 1 hour, gently stirring through twice, before serving.
SERVES 4.

TIPS

* Chinese Five-Spice powder is a fragrant spicy powder made up of ground fennel, pimento, aniseed, cinnamon and cloves.

** Freshly chopped parsley or rosemary can be used in place of the coriander.

◆ This salad may be covered and refrigerated for up to 6 hours, then left at room temperature for 1 hour, before serving.

◆ This salad can be made with new potatoes: boil the unpeeled new potatoes until tender, then pierce all over with a skewer and proceed with step 3.

◆ Add slivers of sun-dried tomatoes steeped in olive oil, seeded and sliced black olives, or capers for a variation.

◆ Use extra-virgin, cold-pressed olive oil for the best quality and flavour. Do not refrigerate, as it will become cloudy.

◆ To get the most juice from a lemon, heat it in a pan of very hot water, or in a moderate oven for 2 minutes, before squeezing.

ITALIAN SALAD PLATTER

Antipasto, an Italian original, is as beautiful to look at as it is delicious to eat. It makes a most colourful start to any meal, and is excellent for parties and buffets. Antipasto can be made up of many different ingredients, but traditionally it always includes a pork product: use Parma ham, mortadella, or salami.

100 g (4 oz) button mushrooms
100 g (4 oz) courgette slices
100 g (4 oz) broccoli florets
250 g (9 oz) salami, Parma ham, or mortadella, thinly sliced
140 g (5 oz) canned butter beans
3 hard-boiled eggs
6 anchovy fillets
100 g (4 oz) Italian black olives
1 each red and green pepper, grilled and marinated (see p. 145)
3 red plum tomatoes
50 g (2 oz) mozzarella cheese, sliced

DRESSING
85 ml (3 fl oz) wine vinegar
2 cloves garlic, crushed
salt and freshly ground black pepper
1 tbsp chopped fresh oregano
1 tbsp chopped fresh basil
1 tbsp chopped fresh thyme
120 ml (4 fl oz) olive oil

1 First make dressing by combining vinegar, garlic, seasoning, herbs and oil.

2 To prepare platter, separately marinate the mushrooms, courgettes and broccoli using three-quarters of the dressing. Set aside.

3 Arrange meat on one section of a large decorative serving platter. Arrange butter beans on the platter and pour remaining dressing over the beans.

4 Quarter each hard-boiled egg. Slice anchovy fillets in half, then carefully wrap a halved fillet around each egg quarter, and arrange on a platter.

5 Place olives and marinated pepper slices on platter.

6 Remove vegetables with a spoon, reserving marinade, and arrange on platter. Pour a little reserved marinade over them.

7 Slice tomatoes. Arrange on platter, alternating each slice of tomato with a slice of mozzarella cheese. Pour over remaining marinade. Serve as a starter with Italian bread.
SERVES 6–8.

TIP

◆ Vary the fresh ingredients to suit seasonal availability.

ICE CREAM WITH CHOCOLATE SAUCE

Never off restaurant dessert menus, this firm favourite is always a winning combination.

ICE CREAM
500 ml (17 fl oz) whipping cream
1 x 397 g can full cream condensed milk
1 tsp vanilla essence
3 extra-large egg whites

CHOCOLATE SAUCE
25 g (1 oz) cocoa powder
75 g (3 oz) light brown sugar
100 ml (3½ fl oz) golden syrup
1 tsp instant coffee powder dissolved in 250 ml (8 fl oz) boiling water
1 tsp vanilla essence
3 tbsp butter
100 g (4 oz) flaked almonds (optional)
wafers for serving

1 To make ice cream, whip cream until it starts to thicken. Add condensed milk and vanilla essence. Beat again.

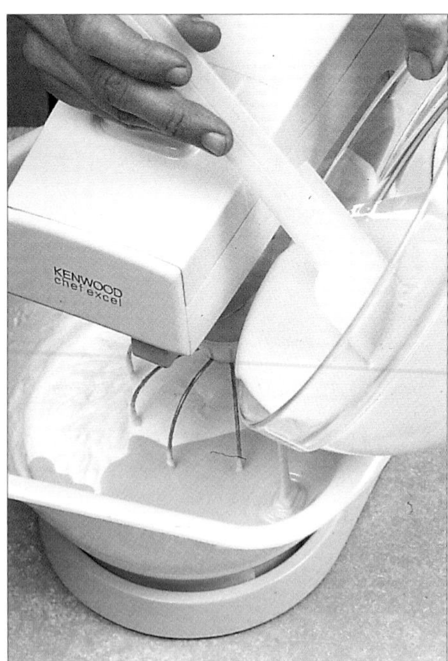

2 Whip egg whites until stiff. If egg whites will not whip up, add a pinch of salt.

3 Fold egg whites into cream mixture in a figure of 8 movement, using a metal spoon. Pour into a 2 litre (3½ pint) plastic container, cover and freeze.

4 Just before it sets solid, remove from the freezer and lightly whip up again. This gives a better texture to the ice cream. Cover and re-freeze.

5 To make chocolate sauce, combine all the ingredients, except the vanilla essence, butter and almonds, in a heavy-based saucepan. Dissolve over a low heat, stirring all the time. Allow to simmer gently for 3 minutes.

6 Remove from heat and add butter and vanilla essence. Stir through to melt butter.

7 Toast almonds, if using, in a pre-heated frying pan with 2 tsp sunflower oil. Stir almonds constantly with a wooden spoon until browned. Sprinkle over individual portions of ice cream and hot chocolate sauce just before serving, and arrange 2–3 wafers on the side of each bowl.

MAKES ABOUT 2 LITRES (3½ PINTS) ICE CREAM AND 500 ML (17 FL OZ) CHOCOLATE SAUCE.

TIP

◆ The chocolate sauce will keep for a long time covered in the refrigerator. Re-heat the sauce in a microwave oven or in the top of a double boiler.

FRUIT CLAFOUTIS

A fruit dessert with French origins using a pancake batter which is poured over stoned fruit and then baked. The darker the fresh fruit, such as cherries and plums, the better the dessert, but canned fruit can be used when cherries and plums are out of season.

750 g ($1\frac{3}{4}$ lb) fruit of your choice (soft plums, cherries, youngberries or raspberries), or 1 x 825 g can of fruit (pear halves, apricots or peach slices)
60 g ($2\frac{1}{2}$ oz) plain flour
$\frac{1}{2}$ tsp baking powder
75 g (3 oz) caster sugar
3 extra-large eggs, beaten
500 ml (17 fl oz) milk
1 tsp vanilla essence
icing sugar, sifted
whipping cream to serve

1 If you are using fresh fruit, wash and stone. Lightly grease a shallow, ovenproof dish with butter.

2 Arrange the prepared fruit in the base of the dish. If using canned fruit, drain well and then arrange in the base of the dish.

3 Sift together the flour, baking powder and caster sugar in a bowl. Combine the eggs, milk and vanilla essence. Make a well in the flour and add the milk and egg mixture.

4 Mix to a smooth batter. Add batter gently to the fruit, by pouring it over the back of a metal spoon. Bake at 200 °C (400 °F/gas 6) for 30–40 minutes. Remove from oven and cool slightly.

5 Sprinkle thickly with sifted icing sugar. Serve hot with whipped cream.
SERVES 4–6.

TIPS

◆ If desired, 3 tbsp brandy or liqueur may be poured over the fruit before the batter is added.

◆ Use eggs that are at room temperature for a lighter result.

◆ To whip up cream perfectly, first chill the cream in the refrigerator and then whip it up in a clean bowl. Use a metal or glass bowl rather than a plastic one. For an even better result, chill the bowl and beaters first.

◆ If cream is overwhipped, it will separate and turn to butter, so take care.

◆ If you do not have caster sugar, make some by processing granulated sugar in a blender for 2 minutes, until it is fine.

HOT CHOCOLATE SAUCE PUDDING

This pudding evokes childhood memories when food was a most important aspect of our family life! Perfect for chilly nights – a spongy pudding with a thick syrupy chocolate sauce, topped with vanilla custard.

4 tbsp butter
125 g (4½ oz) sugar
1 extra-large egg
125 g (4½ oz) self-raising flour
5 tsp cocoa powder
120 ml (4 fl oz) milk

SAUCE
60 g (2½ oz) brown sugar
1 tbsp cocoa powder
375 ml (13 fl oz) boiling water

CUSTARD
1 tsp cornflour
500 ml (17 fl oz) milk
1 tsp vanilla essence
pinch of salt
4 egg yolks
4 tbsp caster sugar

1 To make the pudding, cream together the butter and sugar in a bowl with an electric beater or a wooden spoon. Add the egg to the creamed mixture and then beat together well.

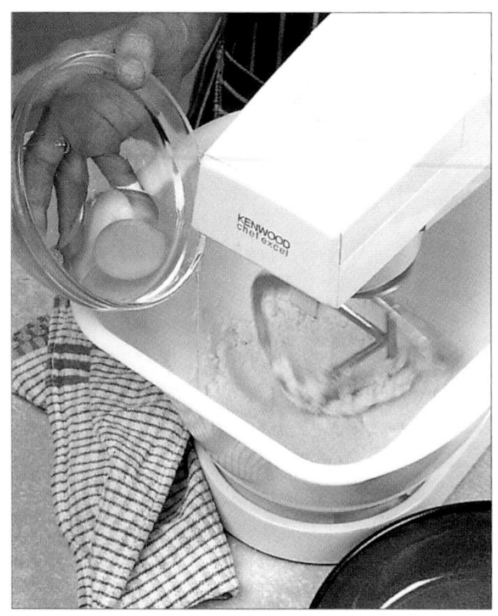

2 Sift together flour and cocoa powder. Add to creamed mixture together with milk. Pour into greased 20 cm (8 in) square, or 2 litre (3½ pint) round, baking dish.

3 To make sauce, dissolve sugar and cocoa in boiling water. Pour the sauce over the back of a metal spoon onto the pudding. Bake for 30 minutes at 180 °C (350 °F/gas 4). Remove from oven, set aside and make custard.

4 To make custard, slake cornflour in 2 tbsp milk. Heat remaining milk, add slaked cornflour, vanilla essence and salt, and bring to a gentle boil.

5 Beat egg yolks and sugar together with metal whisk. Pour warm milk mixture into egg mixture, stirring constantly with a wooden spoon.

6 Pour mixture back into saucepan. Cook over a low heat, stirring constantly with a wooden spoon until it begins to thicken. Pour into a jug, and serve with hot chocolate pudding.
SERVES 6.

TIP

◆ If custard overheats and curdles, remove from heat and beat with electric beater.

CHOCOLATE PROFITEROLES

These choux pastry puffs make an excellent dessert, or are equally good served for tea. Do not fill the profiteroles more than 30 minutes before serving or they may go soggy.

CHOUX PASTRY
250 ml (8 fl oz) water
100 g (4 oz) butter
pinch of salt
150 g (5 oz) plain flour, sifted
3–3$\frac{1}{2}$ lightly beaten, extra-large eggs

FILLING
250 ml (8 fl oz) cream, whipped
3 tbsp icing sugar

SAUCE
4 tbsp brown sugar
3 tbsp water
25 g (1 oz) dark chocolate
1 tbsp cocoa powder
50 g (2 oz) butter
2 tbsp nibbed almonds (optional)

1 To make the profiteroles, place the water, butter and salt in a small saucepan. Bring to the boil and then immediately remove from the heat and add the sifted flour. Return to the heat.

2 Using a wooden spoon, stir over low heat until mixture forms a ball. Remove from heat, place dough in mixing bowl, and allow to cool slightly.

3 Add half the beaten egg to dough and mix with an electric whisk.

4 Add enough extra beaten egg to make a shiny dough that will hold its shape, taking care, as the amount needed varies.

5 Using a piping bag with a 1 cm ($\frac{1}{2}$ in) plain nozzle, pipe into mounds, set well apart, on a greased baking sheet. Bake at 220 °C (425 °F/gas 7) for 10 minutes, then reduce the temperature to 180 °C (350 °F/gas 4) and bake for about 15–20 minutes until golden brown.

6 Remove from oven, turn profiteroles over, and make a slit in the bottom of each one. Turn off oven, return profiteroles to the oven, and allow to dry out for a further 10 minutes. Remove from oven and cool on a rack.

7 To make the filling, combine the whipped cream and icing sugar. Place in a piping bag fitted with a fluted nozzle. Holding the cold profiteroles in one hand, fill from the bottom with cream.

8 To make the chocolate sauce, combine all ingredients except butter and nuts in a pan. Bring the sauce to the boil, stirring constantly. Remove from heat and beat in butter. Cool slightly. Holding profiteroles by the base, dip tops into sauce. Sprinkle with nuts, if using. Allow 2 per person.
MAKES 24–36 PROFITEROLES.

CREPES SUZETTE

This world-famous dessert is usually whipped up with plenty of pomp and splendour in restaurants.

CREPE BATTER
100 g (4 oz) plain flour
pinch of salt
1 tbsp caster sugar
2 extra-large eggs
200 ml (7 fl oz) milk
100 ml ($3^{1}/_{2}$ fl oz) water
1 tbsp melted butter

SAUCE
150 ml (5 fl oz) fresh orange juice
grated rind of 1 orange
grated rind of 1 lemon
1 tbsp caster sugar
7 tbsp Van der Hum, Cointreau or brandy
4 tbsp butter
orange segments and thinly sliced rind to garnish

1 To make the batter, sift flour, salt and sugar into a bowl. Beat eggs lightly. Add milk, water and butter to eggs and beat again.

2 Make a well in the centre of the dry ingredients. Add the beaten egg mixture and, using an electric whisk, beat until the batter is smooth.

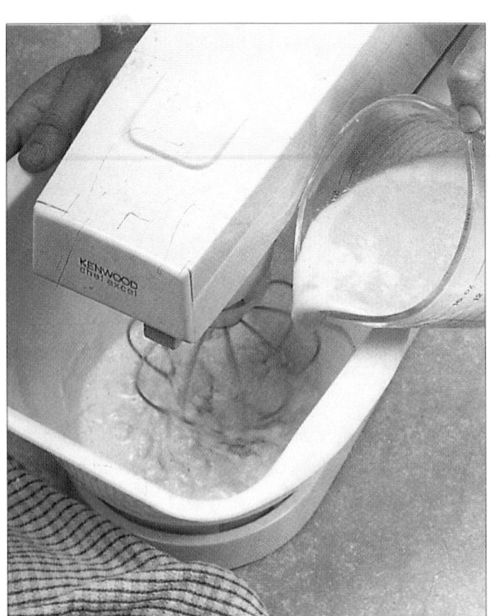

3 Pre-heat a heavy-based, approximately 20 cm (8 in) large, frying pan. Oil the pan lightly and pour in 2 tbsp batter, swirling the pan to coat evenly. Each crêpe will take approximately 1 minute to cook. If they are thin enough, there will be no need to flip them. Fold the completed crêpe in half once, then again, to make a triangle.

4 To make the sauce, combine the orange juice, orange and lemon rind, caster sugar and 4 tbsp of the liqueur or brandy. Melt the butter in a large frying pan (an electric frying pan makes light work of this). Add remaining ingredients and heat through.

5 Add the crêpes to the butter sauce, warming through and turning, allowing the sauce to run into the folds. Garnish, then heat remaining liqueur, pour over the crêpes and flame. Serve at once.
SERVES 6–8.

TIPS

◆ Crêpes freeze very well. Make a pile, stacking the crêpes one on top of the other and placing a piece of cling film between each layer to prevent them from sticking together. Cover well and then freeze.

◆ Crêpes always should be wafer-thin, and can be used to wrap a variety of sweet or savoury fillings of your choice.

◆ To turn a crêpe in the pan very quickly and easily, simply toss it with a quick flip of the wrist, and then brown the other side for a minute or two.

◆ A crêpe pan is very useful in turning out perfect crêpes. They are made of cast iron and should simply be wiped out with absorbent paper after use.

PEARS IN RED WINE

A classic but simple dessert. Fresh pears are available in the winter months and, cooked in red wine, make an excellent and sophisticated end to a wintry meal.

6 large, firm Packham's Triumph pears
750 ml (1 1/4 pints) dry red wine
500 ml (17 fl oz) water
200 g (7 oz) caster sugar
6 whole cloves
1 stick cinnamon
1 bay leaf
strip of lemon rind
strip of orange rind
250 ml (8 fl oz) whipping cream

1 Peel pears carefully, retaining stalks. Trim bases if necessary to allow pears to stand in the pan.

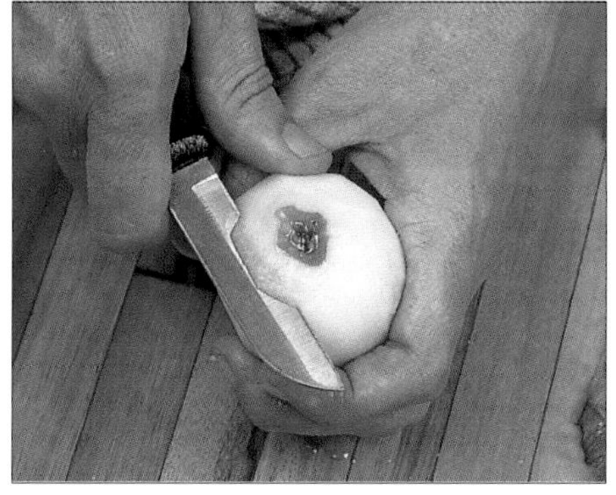

2 Combine wine, water and sugar in a pan. Simmer over low heat, stirring until sugar is dissolved. Add cloves, cinnamon, bay leaf and rinds.

3 Place pears in the syrup and simmer gently for 2–3 hours. Occasionally, gently turn pears using two wooden spoons – metal spoons will make unattractive incisions in the fruit. If the syrup evaporates too quickly, a mixture of water and wine can be added.

4 Once pears are tender, remove from heat and allow to stand in the syrup overnight.

5 Strain off spices from syrup. For a more decorative finish, fan the rounded bases of the pears with a sharp knife. Serve with freshly whipped cream.
SERVES 6.

TIPS

◆ The longer the pears stand in the syrup, the darker the colour and better the flavour will be.

◆ Commonly available varieties of pears include Beurre Hardy, Packham's Triumph, Comice, Williams, Conference and Bosc. Comice, Packham's Triumph and Beurre Hardy are all suitable for cooking.

◆ Pears, like apples, discolour when cut. To prevent this, coat with lemon juice or vinegar.

◆ Pears are picked and sold when they are still hard and unripe. To enjoy a perfectly ripened pear, ripen them in a brown paper bag. Fold the top closed and leave at room temperature. Check daily for ripeness by gently pressing the flesh at the stalk end with your fingers. When the flesh is soft, the pear is ripe and ready to eat.

◆ Pears are nutritious as they are low in calories but exceptionally high in fibre. They also contain valuable minerals like potassium, calcium and phosphorus.

LEMON MERINGUE PIE

The tang of the lemony filling and the sweetness of the meringue combine to make this rich dessert an all-time favourite. Slice into generous wedges and serve on small plates.

PASTRY
4 tbsp butter
100 g (4 oz) caster sugar
1 large egg
1 tsp vanilla essence
125 g (4½ oz) plain flour
1 tsp baking powder

FILLING
1 x 397 g can full cream condensed milk
3 extra-large egg yolks
grated rind of 2 lemons
juice of 3 medium lemons

TOPPING
3 extra-large egg whites
75 g (3 oz) caster sugar
40 g (1½ oz) icing sugar, sifted

1 To make pastry, cream butter and caster sugar. Add egg and vanilla essence, and beat.

2 Sift together the flour and baking powder. Fold into the creamed butter mixture and beat until just combined.

3 Press pastry into a 20 cm (8 in) greased pie dish. Bake blind at 190 °C (375 °F/gas 5) for 15 minutes.

4 To make filling, combine all ingredients. Mix until filling starts to thicken.

5 Pour the filling into the pre-baked pie shell, and bake for a further 10 minutes at 190 °C (375 °F/gas 5).

6 Whip up egg whites until stiff. If they fail to stiffen, add a pinch of salt. Add caster sugar a little at a time, beating constantly.

7 Lastly, fold in sifted icing sugar using a metal spoon.

8 Using a piping bag with a fluted nozzle, pipe swirls of meringue onto the top of the pie. Return to oven and bake at 160 °C (325 °F/gas 3) for a further 5–10 minutes, until meringue starts to brown. Remove from oven and cool, then serve.
SERVES 6.

TIPS

- If you do not have any caster sugar, process granulated sugar for 2 minutes in a food processor using the metal blade.
- This pie looks pretty if baked in a 20 cm (8 in), flute-edged, loose-bottomed flan ring.
- Lightly sprinkle the top of the meringue with sugar before baking, for extra crispness.
- Combine caster sugar with icing sugar for a meringue topping that will keep longer.

CREME BRULEE

A recipe with English origins dating back to the eighteenth century. It is also known as Burnt Cream.

600 ml (1 pint) single cream
6 extra-large egg yolks
4 tsp cornflour
2 tbsp caster sugar
1 tsp vanilla essence
75 g (3 oz) caster sugar

1 Heat cream in a heavy-based saucepan until it just reaches boiling point.

2 Combine egg yolks, cornflour, 2 tbsp caster sugar and vanilla essence in a large mixing bowl. Whisk until smooth.

3 Pour hot cream into egg yolk mixture, whisking constantly. Pour back into saucepan, return to the heat and, stirring constantly, allow mixture to thicken. This will take a few minutes.

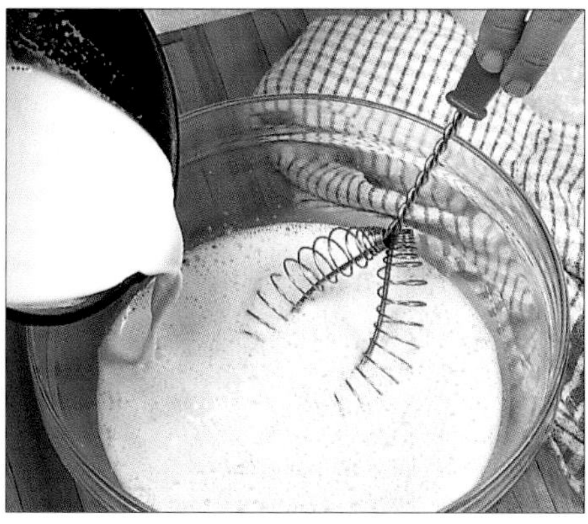

4 Strain mixture into a jug to remove any bits of cooked egg and then pour into individual ramekins. Cover with cling film and refrigerate overnight. This is an essential step.

5 About an hour before serving, sprinkle the top with an even layer of sifted caster sugar. Place ramekins in a baking dish which has been base-lined with a clean, damp cloth, and pack ice cubes around each ramekin.

6 Place under a very hot, pre-heated grill until the sugar melts and caramelizes. It burns easily, so watch carefully. Refrigerate before serving.

7 If desired, crack caramelized, hard top of each dessert with the back of a teaspoon. (Do not refrigerate for long, or the top will go soggy.) Place ramekins on individual plates and serve.
SERVES 6.

TIPS

◆ This dessert can be prepared in one large dish, but I find it easier to handle in individual ramekins.

◆ For a delicious variation, spoon a soft fruit such as raspberries into the base of the ramekins before adding the custard mixture in step 4, then continue as above.

◆ This tip to caramelize the sugar topping easily is gleaned from professional food stylists. If you have access to a small, hand-held, portable gas blow-torch, step 6 (grilling the sugar topping) is made very simple: ignite the blow-torch and carefully melt the sugar topping, taking care not to let it burn. Do this approximately 1 hour before serving. Cover and refrigerate before serving.

LAYERED FRUIT PAVLOVA

This meringue recipe is both economical and very successful.

MERINGUE
2 extra-large egg whites
400 g (14 oz) caster sugar
4 tbsp boiling water
2 tsp white vinegar
1 tsp vanilla essence
2 tsp baking powder

FILLING
fruit in season, e.g. peaches, strawberries, granadilla, kiwi fruit
250 ml (8 fl oz) whipping cream

1 To make meringue, combine all ingredients except baking powder in the large mixing bowl of an electric mixer.

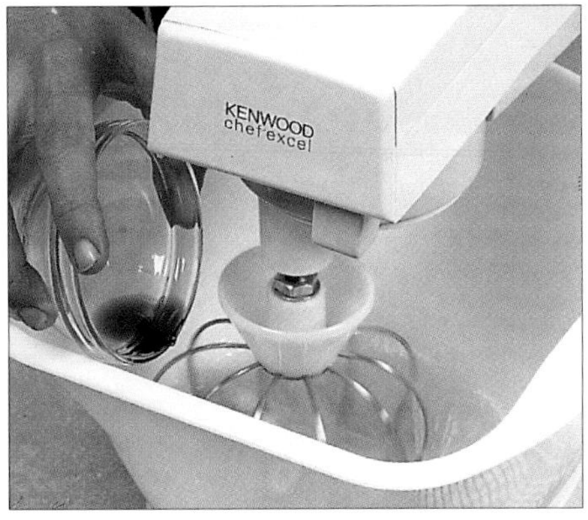

2 Beat until very stiff. This will take approximately 5–7 minutes. Add baking powder and beat for a further minute.

3 Spray a 23 x 32 cm (9 x 13 in) baking sheet with non-stick cooking spray (or see tip). Spread one third of the meringue mixture in a layer on the base of the sheet.

4 Place remaining meringue mixture in a piping bag fitted with a star nozzle. Pipe a thick border around the edge of the meringue base.

5 Bake at 120 °C (250 °F/gas ½) for 2–3 hours. Turn off oven and allow to dry out overnight. Remove and cool completely.

6 To make topping, stone fruit and slice thinly. Dip any fruit that will discolour into lemon juice. Just before serving, spread meringue base with whipped cream, then layer fruit decoratively over the top. Serve immediately. Although the pavlova will keep in the refrigerator for up to 2 hours before serving, the base will become a little soggy.
SERVES 6–8.

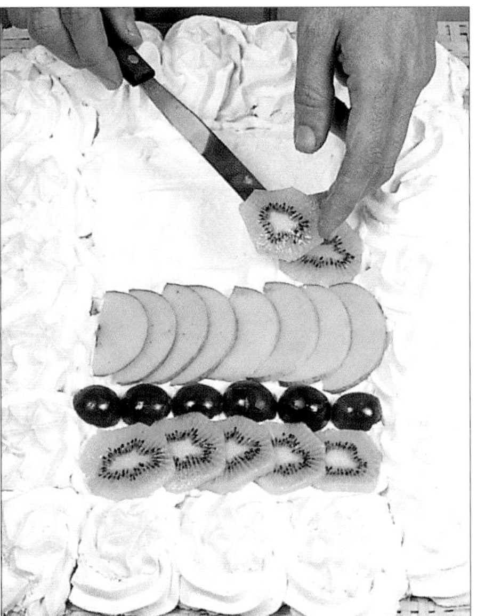

TIPS

- To remove pavlova from the baking sheet easily, first line with an ovenproof baking bag which has been cut in half, making sure that the edges of the bag overlap the baking sheet. Once the meringue is baked, carefully lift the bag off the baking sheet, and, peeling off the bag, slide the meringue onto a platter.
- For individual meringues, pipe swirls onto a large baking sheet with a piping bag, leaving room for spreading. Bake at 120 °C (250 °F/gas ½) for 1 hour. Turn off oven and dry out overnight.

CHOCOLATE MOUSSE

A delicious chocolate mousse, using only cocoa and no chocolate.

5 tsp instant coffee powder
120 ml (4 fl oz) boiling water
200 g (7 oz) caster sugar
60 g (2 oz) cocoa powder
4 extra-large egg yolks
500 ml (17 fl oz) whipping cream
cocoa powder for sprinkling on top

1 Combine instant coffee powder and boiling water in a heavy-based saucepan.

2 Add sugar and cocoa. Stir over low heat until smooth and cocoa is dissolved.

3 Beat egg yolks until thick and light in colour. This can be done by standing mixing bowl over a pan of boiling water, off the hob.

4 Carefully pour the hot, but not boiling, cocoa mixture into the egg yolks to cook them slightly, and combine (if the cocoa is too hot, the eggs will curdle). Cool completely in the refrigerator.

5 Whip 250 ml (8 fl oz) of the cream until thickened. Stir the cooled chocolate mixture into the whipped cream. Pour into individual serving glasses for elegant serving, or into one large glass serving dish if preferred.

6 Cover with cling film and freeze overnight. Remove from the freezer about 30 minutes before serving.

7 Whip the remaining cream until stiff. Cover the chocolate mousse with a blanket of thick cream. Sprinkle the sifted cocoa powder, or fine instant coffee powder, over the top.
SERVES 4–6.

TIPS

- This dessert freezes well: keep well covered in the freezer for up to 6 weeks.

- Decorate the top of the mousse with chocolate leaves. Paint the back of rose leaves, or the tops of nasturtium or geranium leaves, with melted chocolate. Allow to set completely, then carefully peel away the leaf.

- If desired, reduce the amount of cocoa powder for a less concentrated chocolate flavour.

- Use room-temperature egg yolks for extra lightness.

MIXED BERRY COCONUT TART

Perfect as a summer treat when fruit is bountiful and of excellent quality.

BASE
75 g (3 oz) butter
125 g (4½ oz) caster sugar
150 g (5 oz) desiccated coconut
2 extra-large eggs

FILLING
250 g (9 oz) mixed berries in season, e.g. strawberries, cherries or raspberries
3 tbsp caster sugar

SAUCE
250 g (9 oz) fresh, ripe strawberries
4 tbsp caster sugar
2 tbsp brandy or liqueur of choice

TO SERVE
250 ml (8 fl oz) whipping cream

1 To make the base, cream the butter and sugar until light and creamy. Fold the coconut into the creamed mixture.

2 Beat the eggs until thick and light in colour. Fold into the creamed coconut mixture, using a metal spoon.

3 Spray a 23 cm (9 in) loose-bottomed tin with non-stick cooking spray. Spread creamed coconut mixture into base of tin. Place tin on a baking sheet. Bake at 180 °C (350 °F/gas 4) for 20 minutes, until set and golden brown. (A little oil from the butter may spill out onto the baking sheet.) Remove from oven, cool for 2 minutes,then use spatula to loosen the bottom.

4 To make filling, wash fruit, hull strawberries and remove stones from cherries. Sprinkle with sugar and set aside.

5 To make strawberry sauce, hull strawberries, slice and place in a pan with sugar and brandy. Bring to a slow boil.

6 Place in a food processor and process until smooth.

7 Pile whipped cream on cooled tart base, scatter fruit on top of cream. Pour a little sauce into a serving dish. Place slice of tart on top of sauce and serve, or serve sauce separately.
SERVES 6.

TIP

◆ This dessert looks spectacular served on a pedestal dish dusted with icing sugar.

A GOOD FRUIT LOAF

This simple, light-coloured fruit loaf is packed full with cherries and fruit.

500 g (18 oz) mixed dried fruit (sultanas, raisins, currants, mixed peel)
125 g (4½ oz) glacé cherries*
1 tbsp plain flour
125 g (4½ oz) butter**
200 g (7 oz) caster sugar
4 extra-large eggs
250 g (9 oz) plain flour
½ tsp baking powder

1 Place mixed dried fruit in pan, add water to just cover, bring to the boil and boil for 20 minutes.

2 Rinse mixed dried fruit in colander, cool, and drain well. Add whole cherries. Stir 1 tbsp flour into the cooled fruit.

3 Cream butter and sugar until light and fluffy. Add eggs one at a time, mixing well after each addition.

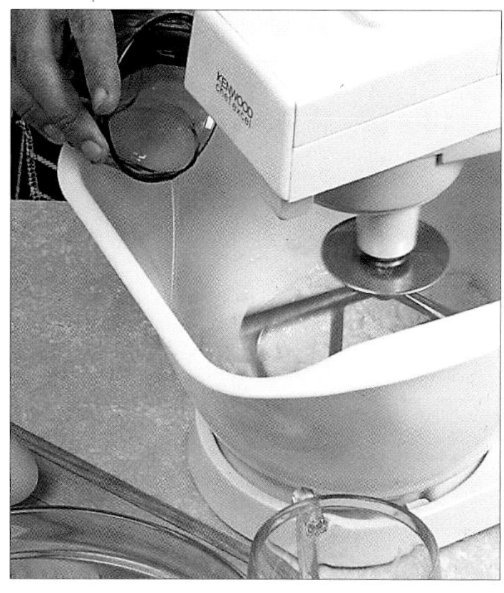

4 Sift together flour and baking powder. Add to creamed mixture, mixing well. Fold in mixed dried fruit.

5 Grease a 10 x 28 cm (4 x 11 in) loaf tin. Spoon in mixture and bake at 180 °C (350 °F/gas 4) for 1 hour. Test with a skewer and, if still very wet, reduce temperature to 160 °C (325 °F/gas 3) and bake for a further 15 minutes.

6 Remove from oven and cool in tin for 5 minutes, then turn out onto a rack to cool competely. Dust with sifted icing sugar before serving.
MAKES 15 GENEROUS SLICES.

TIPS

* Green cherries may be used for a colourful alternative.

** Do not attempt to make this loaf with margarine – the taste will not be the same.

◆ To help the loaf keep longer, fold in 85 ml (3 fl oz) brandy with the mixed dried fruit in step 4.

◆ 100 g (4 oz) chopped nuts, such as almonds, pecan nuts, walnuts or brazil nuts, can be added with the mixed dried fruit in step 4.

◆ This loaf does not keep well and should be eaten within a few days of baking. Store well wrapped in an airtight container.

CRUNCHIES WITH CHOCOLATE TOPPING

Perfect lunch box fillers.

125 g (4½ oz) plain flour
100 g (4 oz) rolled oats
100 g (4 oz) desiccated coconut
200 g (7 oz) caster sugar
125 g (4½ oz) butter
2 tbsp golden syrup
1 tsp bicarbonate of soda
2 tbsp boiling water

ICING
175 g (6 oz) icing sugar
4 tsp cocoa
4 tsp butter, melted
a little boiling water

1 To make crunchies, combine flour, oats, coconut and sugar in a large mixing bowl.

2 Combine butter and syrup in a pot. Melt over low heat. Do not allow to boil.

3 Dissolve bicarbonate of soda in boiling water. Add to melted butter and syrup.

4 Add to dry ingredients and combine. Press into a greased 33 x 23 cm (13 x 9 in) baking sheet. Bake at 160 °C (325 °F/gas 3) for 30 minutes.

5 To make icing, sift icing sugar and cocoa together. Add melted butter and enough boiling water 1 tbsp at a time, as the icing can become runny very quickly, to make an icing of a thick pouring consistency.

6 Remove crunchies from oven, and cool for 5 minutes. Spread chocolate icing on hot crunchies. Leave to cool slightly and cut into squares, then turn out onto a rack to cool completely. Store in an airtight container.
MAKES APPROXIMATELY 36 SQUARES.

TIPS

◆ 75 g (3 oz) raisins or nuts can be added in step 1 to make a more interesting crunchie.

◆ The chocolate icing can be omitted if desired.

◆ To make a 'health crunchie', add sunflower seeds, sesame seeds and linseeds. Replace 100 g (4 oz) desiccated coconut with 3 tbsp sunflower seeds mixed with 3 tbsp sesame seeds, 3 tbsp linseeds, and 6 tbsp desiccated coconut.

◆ These crunchies freeze well.

◆ Replace the plain flour with wholemeal flour if preferred.

CHOCOLATE CHIP MUFFINS

Rich, dark and chocolaty – these are certainly an interesting addition to the muffin repertoire.

350 g (12 oz) plain flour
40 g (1½ oz) cocoa powder
1 tbsp baking powder
½ tsp salt
175 g (6 oz) caster sugar
200 g (7 oz) chocolate chips
2 extra-large eggs, separated, plus 2 extra egg whites
350 ml (12 fl oz) buttermilk, plain yoghurt, or sour milk
175 g (6 oz) butter, melted and cooled

1 Pre-heat oven to 200 °C (400 °F/gas 6). Sift flour, cocoa, baking powder and salt twice into a bowl.

2 Stir in sugar and chocolate chips. In another bowl, beat egg yolks with buttermilk, yoghurt or sour milk, and melted butter.

3 In a third bowl, stiffly whisk egg whites. Stir buttermilk mixture into flour mixture, then carefully fold in the stiffly beaten egg whites.

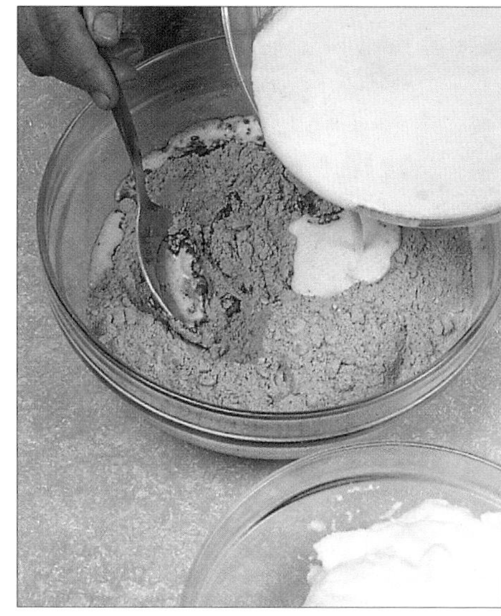

4 Spoon batter into greased muffin tins, filling each two-thirds full. Bake for 20 minutes. Leave in tin for 2 minutes, then remove to cooling rack.

5 Eat the muffins while they are still warm, with plenty of freshly whipped cream.
MAKES 18 MUFFINS.

TIPS

◆ These Chocolate Chip Muffins keep and freeze well.

◆ For an interesting variation, use half chocolate, half butterscotch chips or chopped walnuts.

◆ It is important not to over-mix muffin mixtures once the wet and dry ingredients have been combined. Over-mixing creates air tunnels in the muffins, which cause them to rise unevenly.

◆ If you don't want to use chocolate chips, use a slab of dark chocolate and grate.

◆ To make sour milk, add 1 tbsp lemon juice or white vinegar to 250 ml (8 fl oz) milk. Stir well and stand for 10 minutes before using.

◆ If you would prefer a sweeter, lighter muffin, use 25 g (1 oz) cocoa powder and increase sugar to 200 g (7 oz).

◆ Replace the chocolate chips with raisins if preferred.

◆ Store baking powder in a tightly sealed, airtight container.

CHOCOLATE CAKE

This rich, layered cake with delicious butter icing is a universal favourite.

250 ml (8 fl oz) boiling water
50 g (2 oz) cocoa powder
60 g (2½ oz) dark chocolate, broken into pieces
1 tsp vanilla essence
4 extra-large eggs, separated
120 ml (4 fl oz) oil
250 g (9 oz) plain flour
pinch of salt
300 g (11 oz) caster sugar
1 tbsp baking powder

BUTTER ICING
2 tbsp cocoa
500 g (18 oz) icing sugar
125 g (4½ oz) butter, softened
1 extra-large egg, beaten
1 tsp vanilla essence

1 To make cake, combine boiling water, cocoa and chocolate. Stir to dissolve, and allow to cool slightly.

2 Combine chocolate mixture with vanilla essence, egg yolks and oil. Sift flour, salt, caster sugar and baking powder together, and make a well in the centre of these dry ingredients.

3 Beat chocolate mixture well, and add to dry ingredients. Mix to combine.

4 Beat the egg whites with a pinch of salt until stiff, then fold into the chocolate mixture with a metal spoon in a figure of 8 movement, taking care not to over-beat.

5 Spray a 23 cm (9 in) round cake tin with non-stick cooking spray. Pour mixture into tin and bake at 190 °C (375 °F/gas 5) for 45 minutes, or until firm to the touch. Stand in tin for 5 minutes before removing to rack to cool.

6 While the cake is cooling, make icing. Sift together cocoa and sugar, add butter, and cream together with electric whisk. Mix in egg and vanilla essence.

7 Cut cooled cake in half horizontally, by inserting the blade of a knife into the centre of the cake, and turning the cake to obtain two equal halves. Sandwich layers together with icing and ice the top and sides using a round-bladed knife or spatula, dipped into hot water before each smear. Store in an airtight container.
MAKES 1 LARGE CAKE.

TIPS

◆ This cake freezes well – open freeze until it is solid, then wrap and re-freeze.

◆ Chocolate can be replaced by carob, which is available from health-food stores. The advantages of carob are that it contains no caffeine, is very low in fat, and is also very sweet. The ripe pods of the carob tree are ground to a powder (after the seeds are removed), and this powder can be used in any recipe which calls for cocoa or chocolate. 3 tbsp carob powder mixed with 2 tbsp milk or water is equal to 1 x 2 cm (¾ in) square of chocolate.

SCONES

The baking of good scones is a fundamental skill for any cook. After trying and testing numerous recipes, this is definitely my favourite.

250 g (9 oz) plain flour
4 tsp baking powder
2 tbsp caster sugar
4 tbsp butter
150 ml (5 fl oz) buttermilk
1 extra-large egg
milk to glaze

TO SERVE
120 ml (4 fl oz) whipping cream
1 tbsp caster sugar
1 tsp vanilla essence
jam of your choice

1 Sift flour, baking powder and caster sugar into a bowl. Rub in butter with fingertips, until mixture resembles breadcrumbs.

2 Lightly beat together buttermilk and egg.

3 Pour buttermilk mixture into flour mixture, and bring dough together with a round-bladed knife.

4 On a floured surface, shape dough into a 3 cm (1¼ in) thick rectangle. Using a glass or a cookie cutter with a 6 cm (2½ in) diameter, cut out rounds. A fluted cutter makes a pretty edge.

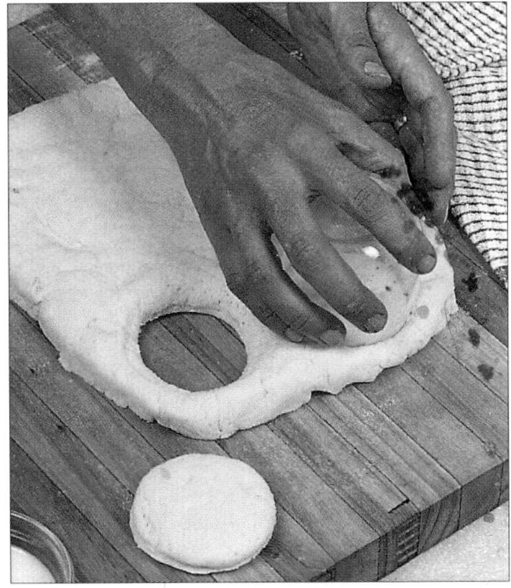

5 Place on a greased baking sheet. Brush lightly with milk and stand for 15 minutes. This step allows baking powder to start activating, and improves the volume of the scones.

6 Bake at 220 °C (425 °F/gas 7) for 10 minutes, or until golden brown. Cool on a rack before splitting.

7 Whip the cream with sugar and vanilla essence. Pipe or spoon a circle of cream on outer edge of the halved scones. Spoon a dollop of jam into the centre and serve.
MAKES 6–8 SCONES.

TIPS

◆ Add some grated lemon or orange rind for a citrus flavour.

◆ Milk may be used instead of buttermilk, although buttermilk gives scones a distinct lightness.

◆ Mixed dried fruit can be added to make a fruit scone. Add 100 g (4 oz) mixed dried fruit (raisins, sultanas and currants) to the crumbed mixture at the end of step 1. A little extra milk or buttermilk may be required to bind the mixture.

◆ To make a wholemeal scone, replace half the plain flour with wholemeal flour.

◆ Scones are best eaten immediately after they are removed from the oven.

CARROT CAKE

This cake is literally packed full of goodness – pineapple, carrots, apple, nuts, raisins. This mixture makes two loaves, one large, 23 cm (9 in) cake, or one bundt shape (cake tin with a funnel in the centre and decorative pattern on the outside).

3 extra-large eggs
200 g (7 oz) caster sugar
100 g (4 oz) light brown sugar
250 ml (8 fl oz) sunflower oil
250 ml (8 fl oz) canned crushed pineapple, well drained
3 carrots, peeled and finely grated
1 large Granny Smith apple, peeled and finely grated
50 g (2 oz) desiccated coconut
100 g (4 oz) walnuts or pecan nuts, chopped
250 g (9 oz) plain flour
2 tsp bicarbonate of soda
1 tsp baking powder
2 tsp ground cinnamon
½ tsp grated nutmeg
75 g (3 oz) raisins or sultanas

CREAM CHEESE ICING
60 g (2 oz) softened butter
250 g (9 oz) icing sugar, sifted
60 g (2 oz) cream cheese
1 tbsp fresh orange juice

1 Put eggs into the bowl of a food processor fitted with a metal blade, and add sugars. Beat on full speed for 2 minutes.

2 While the processor is running, add oil through the feed tube, and mix for a further minute.

3 Add pineapple, carrots, apple, coconut and nuts. Mix for 1 minute.

4 Sift all dry ingredients together in a large mixing bowl. Add carrot mixture, and mix together with a wooden spoon. Stir in raisins or sultanas.

5 Pour into a greased tin of your choice. Bake at 180 °C (350 °F/gas 4) for 60–80 minutes. Remove from oven.

6 Cool in the tin for 5 minutes, then turn out onto a rack. Cool completely before icing.

7 To make icing, combine butter and sugar in a bowl with a wooden spoon. Mix in enough cream cheese to reach a spreading consistency. Add orange juice. Ice cake, and top with orange peel.

TIPS

◆ Because of the cream cheese icing, store the Carrot Cake covered in the refrigerator.

◆ This Carrot Cake freezes well: open freeze until solid, then wrap and re-freeze.

BANANA GINGER LOAF

An interesting combination of flavours that makes a large, delicious loaf. It is much better if eaten on the second day. Store in an airtight container.

300 g (11 oz) plain flour
4 tsp ground ginger
1 tsp ground cinnamon
1 tsp mixed spice
2½ tsp baking powder
pinch of salt
200 g (7 oz) soft butter
200 g (7 oz) soft brown sugar
4 large eggs
6 medium, well-ripened bananas, mashed
120 ml (4 fl oz) milk
2 tbsp golden syrup, or reserved ginger syrup
4 tbsp chopped crystallized ginger, or stem ginger in syrup, drained and syrup reserved

1 Sift the flour, ginger, cinnamon, mixed spice, baking powder and salt together into the bowl of an electric mixer.

2 Add the butter, brown sugar and eggs to the sifted dry ingredients. Beat thoroughly until well blended.

3 Add bananas, milk and syrup and combine. Fold in chopped ginger.

4 Pour batter into a 10 x 28 cm (4 x 11 in) loaf tin. Bake at 160 °C (325 °F/gas 3) for about 45–60 minutes. If the loaf browns too quickly, reduce temperature to 150 °C (300 °F/gas 2). Remove from oven. Cool in tin for 5 minutes, then turn out onto cooling rack and cool completely.
MAKES 1 LARGE LOAF

TIPS

◆ It is essential to use well-ripened bananas or the banana flavour will not be strong enough to permeate the loaf.

◆ To speed up the ripening of bananas, store them for a few days in a warm place or wrap them in newspaper. Bananas keep better if stored in a bunch.

◆ Serve the loaf with this icing:

125 g (4½ oz) icing sugar
2 tbsp lemon juice
boiling water
slices of glacé ginger

Sift the icing sugar into a mixing bowl. Add the lemon juice, and then add the boiling water 1 tsp at a time, taking care as the icing can quickly become a runny mess if you add too much water. Pour the icing over the Banana Ginger Loaf and decorate with thin slices of glacé ginger.

◆ Use freshly ground spices as they have the most flavour. Ground spices lose their flavour if stored for too long so buy in small quantities as needed.

CRUMPETS

These North American favourites, also known as drop scones, griddle cakes or pancakes, are the best things to cheer up a chilly afternoon. Eat them immediately, smothered with butter and honey or syrup.

250 g (9 oz) plain flour
1½ tsp baking powder
pinch of salt
3 tbsp caster sugar
3 large eggs, beaten
450 ml (15 fl oz) full cream milk
4 tbsp butter
oil for frying

1 Sift flour, baking powder, salt and sugar together into a large mixing bowl.

2 Beat together the eggs and the milk.

3 Make a well in the centre of the dry ingredients. Pour egg and milk mixture into this well, and combine using a wooden spoon. The batter will be a little lumpy.

4 Melt the butter, and then stir it into the beaten egg and milk mixture.

5 Cover and refrigerate for 30 minutes. This allows the batter to thicken.

6 Pre-heat a frying pan. Pour in a little oil. Pour off the excess, and spoon on about 1 tbsp of batter per crumpet, allowing room for spreading.

7 The crumpet is ready to turn when bubbles appear on the surface. Re-oil the pan after each batch of crumpets, pouring off excess oil. Serve with plenty of butter, syrup or honey.

MAKES 4–6 GENEROUS SERVINGS.

TIPS

◆ Crumpets are a favourite for an American breakfast: try them served with honey and bacon.

◆ To make wholemeal crumpets, replace half the plain flour with wholemeal flour.

◆ Use buttermilk instead of milk for a lighter result.

◆ Serve the crumpets in an attractive stack – put a small block of butter and a dribble of syrup or honey between each crumpet, and pile them one on top of another. Re-heat the stack just before serving.

◆ Honey is a natural substance made by bees from the nectar of flowers. It is a very nourishing sweetener, filled with minerals and vitamins. Honey is sweeter than sugar, so less can be used.

◆ To make delicious savoury snacks, top each cooled crumpet with thinly sliced smoked salmon, squeeze a little lemon juice over, and sprinkle with freshly ground black pepper.

CHRISTMAS CAKE

This recipe and I have come a long way. It is handwritten on a scrappy piece of paper, yellowed with age and smeared with titbits of cake mixture, and makes a good Christmas, christening or wedding cake. It is best to make the Christmas cake in October, for a well-matured flavour.

200 g (7 oz) brown sugar
250 ml (8 fl oz) water
500 g (18 oz) mixed dried fruit
100 g (4 oz) dried apricots, finely chopped
125 g (4½ oz) butter
1½ tsp bicarbonate of soda
125 g (4½ oz) glacé cherries
100 g (4 oz) pecan nuts, chopped
50 g (2 oz) preserved ginger, chopped
100 g (4 oz) dates, chopped
60 g (2½ oz) mixed glacé fruit (e.g. figs, pears, pineapple), finely chopped
2 extra-large eggs, lightly beaten
250 g (9 oz) plain flour
2 tsp baking powder
1 tsp salt
1 tsp ground cinnamon
½ tsp ground ginger
1 tsp ground nutmeg
4 tbsp brandy
250 ml (8 fl oz) brandy

1 Combine sugar, water, mixed dried fruit, apricots, butter and bicarbonate of soda in a large pan over medium heat. Do not boil until sugar has dissolved. Simmer for 20 minutes, and cool.

2 Add cherries, nuts, ginger, dates and glacé fruit to mixture, and then add eggs.

3 Sift together all dry ingredients, and add to the boiled fruit mixture. Add 4 tbsp brandy and mix well.

4 Prepare a 20 cm (8 in) square or 23 cm (9 in) round cake tin by greasing and lining with non-stick baking paper.

5 Spoon mixture into cake tin, and bake at 150 °C (300 °F/gas 2) for 2–3 hours.

6 Cool cake in tin for approximately 15 minutes before removing to cooling rack. Pour over remaining 250 ml (8 fl oz) brandy, cover with foil, and store for Christmas. Sprinkle cake with up to 120 ml (4 fl oz) brandy each month.

MAKES 1 LARGE CAKE.

TIP

◆ This cake may be studded with glacé cherries and nuts before baking, or iced with Royal Icing 1 week before eating if you wish. Heat 2 tbsp apricot jam and spread over cake with a pastry brush. Roll out 750 g (1¾ lb) marzipan on a surface dusted lightly with icing sugar. Roll into a circle large enough to cover the whole cake. Smooth the marzipan onto the cake with hands dusted with icing sugar. Cover with a clean cloth and leave to dry out for 24 hours. Lightly whisk 2 extra-large egg whites. Gradually add 500 g (18 oz) icing sugar, beating well with a wooden spoon. Add 1 tsp lemon juice. Spread evenly over the marzipan with a spatula.

DEVONSHIRE CREAM CAKE

This is an excellent basic sponge cake which comes up trumps every time. It does not keep well, and is therefore best baked and eaten on the same day. It does, however, freeze well.

5 extra-large eggs
200 g (7 oz) caster sugar
grated rind and juice of 1 lemon
100 g (4 oz) plain flour
50 g (2 oz) cornflour
pinch of salt

FILLING
250 ml (8 fl oz) whipping cream
75 g (3 oz) icing sugar

TOPPING
40 g (1½ oz) cocoa powder
100 g (4 oz) icing sugar
boiling water

1 Pre-heat the oven to 180 °C (350 °F/gas 4). Lightly grease a 23 cm (9 in) round baking tin, or spray with non-stick cooking spray.

2 Separate the yolks from the egg whites and beat the whites until stiff but not dry. Gradually beat in half the caster sugar.

3 Beat egg yolks, lemon rind and juice until fluffy and light, then gradually beat in remaining sugar. Continue beating until mixture is thick and creamy.

4 Fold the egg white mixture into the egg yolk mixture.

5 Sift the flour, cornflour and salt together twice, fold into the egg mixture, and then pour into the prepared tin.

6 Bake for 40–50 minutes. Remove from oven and leave in tin for 5 minutes, then turn out onto a rack and cool completely.

7 To make filling, beat cream and icing sugar together until thick.

8 Slice cake in half horizontally. Sandwich cake halves together with filling.

9 To make topping, sift together cocoa powder and icing sugar. Mix with the boiling water to get a fairly runny glaze. Stand to thicken, then pour over the cake, allowing the icing to drip down the sides.

MAKES APPROXIMATELY 8–10 SLICES.

CHILLED CHEESECAKE

An easy, no-bake version of traditional baked cheesecake. Topped with fresh fruit in season, such as kiwi slices, strawberries or orange slices, this cheesecake looks like a million dollars.

BASE
25 ginger biscuits
1 tsp ground ginger
100 g (4 oz) butter or margarine

FILLING
5 tsp gelatine
4 tbsp water
500 g (18 oz) full-cream cream cheese
finely grated rind and juice of 1 medium orange, or large lemon
1 tsp vanilla essence
3 extra-large egg yolks
200 g (7 oz) caster sugar
250 ml (8 fl oz) cream, lightly whipped
fruit to decorate

1 To make base, crumble biscuits in a food processor using a metal blade. Add ground ginger.

2 Melt butter or margarine, and stir into crumbs. Press a thin layer of the biscuit mixture into the bottom of a greased 23 cm (9 in) loose-bottomed cake tin. Cover and refrigerate while preparing filling.

3 To make filling, sprinkle gelatine into water and allow to sponge.

4 Beat cream cheese, add orange or lemon rind and juice, and vanilla essence.

5 Beat the egg yolks and caster sugar until light in colour and thickened, and add to cream cheese mixture. Add lightly whipped cream.

6 Soften gelatine sponge in microwave on Medium for 2 minutes, or dissolve over a pan of boiling water, off the heat.

7 Add the gelatine in a steady stream to the cream cheese mixture. Whisk through until evenly distributed. Pour into the biscuit base. Refrigerate until set – 3–5 hours or overnight. Decorate with slices of fruit in season.
MAKES 8–10 GENEROUS SLICES.

TIPS

- Replace the cream cheese with Ricotta cheese to reduce the fat content of the cheesecake.
- Gelatine is an extract of the animal protein, collagen. It is available in a powder form or in brittle sheets, and on its own is tasteless. It is simple to use, and will set almost anything except fresh pineapple and pawpaw, which contain an enzyme that prevents gelatine from setting. Cooked or canned pineapple or pawpaw can be used, however.
- Don't freeze gelatine mixtures, as they crystallize and separate.
- Sliced strawberries are very good with this cheesecake.

HOT CROSS BUNS

Traditional fare for Easter Sunday.

500 g (18 oz) plain flour
1 tsp salt
1 tbsp ground cinnamon
2 tsp ground ginger
1½ tsp ground nutmeg
1 tsp mixed spice
½ tsp ground cloves
100 g (4 oz) caster sugar
1 tbsp instant yeast
150 g (5 oz) mixed dried fruit (raisins, sultanas, currants, peel)
200 ml (7 fl oz) milk
100 g (4 oz) butter
2 extra-large eggs

CROSS MIXTURE
100 g (4 oz) plain flour
½ tsp salt
3 tbsp oil
120 ml (4 fl oz) milk

GLAZE
3 tbsp clear honey, warmed

1 Sift together the flour and all the spices in a large mixing bowl. Stir in the sugar and instant yeast. Add the mixed dried fruit.

2 Warm milk to blood temperature. Add butter to milk, and melt. Lightly beat eggs, and add to milk mixture.

3 Pour the milk mixture over the dry ingredients and mix to a soft dough, adding more warmed milk if necessary.

4 Place on a lightly floured surface and knead for 5 minutes. Place in a lightly oiled mixing bowl, cover with a cloth, and put in a warm place for approximately 2 hours, or until risen and doubled in size.

5 Knock down dough, then pinch off pieces about the size of an egg. Roll into a rounded shape in the palm of the hand. Place slightly apart (to allow buns to rise) on a 30 x 23 cm (12 x 9 in) greased baking sheet.

6 Cover with a cloth, and put in a warm place to rise for 15–30 minutes.

7 Just before baking, prepare cross mixture by sifting together flour and salt. Combine oil and milk, and add to flour to make a soft dough. Place in a strong plastic bag, snip off the corner, and pipe crosses on buns. Work in a continuous line across the buns in one direction, and then in the other; do not lift between each bun.

8 Bake at 180 °C (350 °F/gas 4) for 25–30 minutes until golden brown. Cool for 5 minutes and then brush with warmed honey. Hot Cross Buns are best served straight from the oven with plenty of butter.
MAKES 12 BUNS.

TIPS

- A glaze of sifted icing sugar and a little water or milk can be used instead of honey.
- Hot Cross Buns can be frozen for up to 3 months.

NO-NONSENSE HEALTH LOAF

This batter bread requires no kneading. It is a wholesome loaf that can be produced quickly and simply... and it's full of goodness too! The best part of the loaf is its versatility: the flour mixture can be altered to suit what is in the store cupboard; seeds can be changed or omitted, to taste.

15 g (½ oz) fresh yeast
1 tsp sugar
150 ml (5 fl oz) warm water
1 tbsp white bread flour
250 ml (8 fl oz) milk or sour milk
1 tbsp honey
85 ml (3 fl oz) oil
2–3 tsp salt
250 g (9 oz) wholemeal flour
125 g (4½ oz) white bread flour
100 g (4 oz) oats
3 tbsp sesame seeds
3 tbsp sunflower seeds
3 tbsp linseeds
4 tbsp crushed wheat

1 Crumble yeast into a large mixing bowl. Sprinkle sugar over yeast and pour in warm water. Stir to dissolve yeast. Sprinkle 1 tbsp white bread flour on top of yeast mixture, cover, and stand in a warm place.

2 The yeast mixture must always become frothy. If it does not froth, the yeast is inactive and it is necessary to start again with fresh yeast.

3 Warm the milk or sour milk, then add the honey, oil and salt. Combine with the prepared yeast mixture.

4 Add wholemeal flour, white bread flour and oats. Stir through. Add seeds and crushed wheat, and stir with a wooden spoon until seeds are evenly distributed. The mixture should form a thickish batter.

5 Pour into a 10 x 28 cm (4 x 11 in) large, greased loaf tin. Cover with a clean cloth, and put in a warm place for 1 hour, until risen. If desired, more seeds can be sprinkled on top before baking: wet surface with water before sprinkling with seeds.

6 Bake at 190 °C (375 °F/gas 5) for 30 minutes. Remove from the oven and cool in the tin for 5 minutes, then turn out onto a wire rack to cool completely.
MAKES 1 LARGE LOAF.

TIPS

◆ The fresh yeast can be replaced by either 2 tsp dry yeast granules, or by 1½ tsp instant yeast. Follow the directions below:

- For the dry yeast method, omit step 1, combine 2 tsp dry yeast granules, 1 tsp sugar and 1 tsp plain flour with 150 ml (5 fl oz) warm water. Leave to stand in a warm place for about 10–15 minutes, until the yeast mixture becomes frothy. (If it does not froth, the yeast is inactive and you must begin again with fresh yeast.) Continue with step 2.
- For the instant yeast method, omit steps 1 and 2. In step 3, add 150 ml (5 fl oz) water to the milk or sour milk. In step 4, add 1½ tsp instant yeast to wholemeal flour, white bread flour and oats, then proceed with step 4 as above.

◆ To make sour milk, add 1 tbsp lemon juice or vinegar to 250 ml (8 fl oz) milk. Stir well, and leave to stand for about 10 minutes.

◆ To test when a loaf is done, turn out of the tin and tap the bottom – it should sound hollow.

BUTTERMILK ROLLS

Buttermilk or sour milk can be used to make these excellent dinner rolls which have a very good flavour.

500 g (18 oz) white bread flour
1 tsp salt
2 tsp sugar
1 tbsp instant yeast
300 ml (10 fl oz) buttermilk or sour milk
2 tbsp butter
1 extra-large egg, beaten
1 egg beaten with ½ tsp salt and 1 tbsp water, to egg wash rolls before baking

1 Sift the flour and salt into a large bowl. Sprinkle in the sugar and yeast, and stir to mix through the flour.

2 Warm the buttermilk or sour milk, then melt the butter into the warm milk. Add the beaten egg to the milk mixture.

3 Add the milk mixture to flour, and mix to a soft dough.

4 Knead the dough on a lightly floured surface for 5 minutes. Place in lightly oiled bowl, cover, and put in a warm place to rise until doubled in size. This will take approximately 1 hour.

5 Knock back risen dough and knead for 1 minute. Roll out to 2 cm (¾ in) thickness and cut into 8 cm (3¼ in) lengths. Cut lengths into 3 cm (1¼ in) wide strips. Taper ends, and place on greased baking sheet with space between each roll.

6 Cover, and leave to rise for 15 minutes. Brush with egg wash. Bake at 220 °C (425 °F/gas 7) for 10–15 minutes. Remove from the oven and cool on a rack.
MAKES APPROXIMATELY 25 DINNER ROLLS.

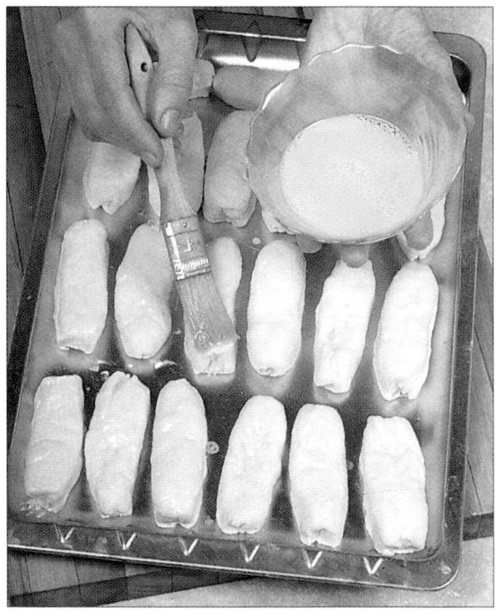

TIPS

◆ Plain flour can replace the white bread flour if preferred.

◆ To make delicious and decorative cocktail snacks, cut a V-shaped groove out of the centre of the rolls and fill with the following combinations:
- shredded lettuce, cream cheese, chives and slivers of tomato
- shredded lettuce, scrambled egg and watercress
- shredded lettuce, smoked beef and mustard

◆ This dough is perfect for normal size rolls: simply divide dough into 50 g (2 oz) pieces and shape into smooth, round balls, brush with egg wash, and bake at 200 °C (400 °F/gas 6) for 20 minutes. Remove from the oven and cool on a rack.

PIZZA

The Italian original with worldwide popularity.

PIZZA BASE
2 tsp active dry yeast
1 tsp sugar
250 ml (8 fl oz) warm water
1 tbsp white bread flour
300 g (11 oz) white bread flour
2 tsp salt

TOPPING
1 x 400 g can whole peeled tomatoes, preferably Italian
1 tbsp tomato paste
1 plump clove garlic, crushed
1 tsp dried basil
1 tsp dried oregano
1 tsp sugar
salt and freshly ground black pepper
300 g (11 oz) mozzarella cheese, grated
toppings of your choice, e.g. salami, mushrooms, tuna, green and red pepper, ham, sliced onion, olives, shrimps, asparagus
1 tbsp grated Parmesan cheese

1 Dissolve yeast and sugar in warm water in a large mixing bowl. Sprinkle with 1 tbsp flour, cover with a cloth and put in a warm place for approximately 10 minutes, until frothy. If it does not froth, start again with a new pack of yeast.

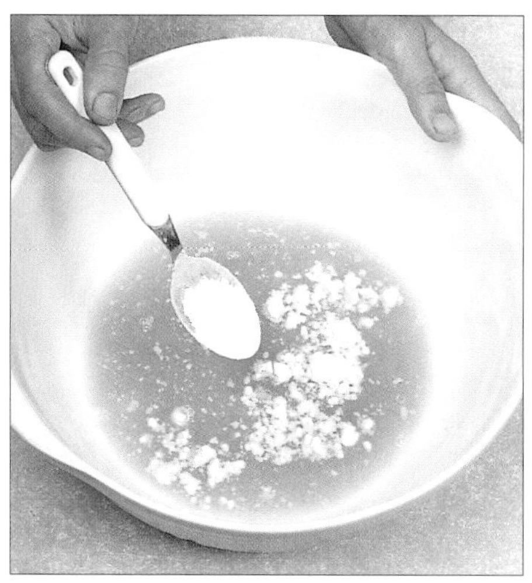

2 Sift 250 g (9 oz) flour and salt over yeast mixture. Stir with a wooden spoon to form a soft dough, adding remaining flour as necessary.

3 Knead on a lightly floured surface for 5 minutes. Place in a lightly oiled bowl, cover, and put in a warm place until doubled in size. This will take approximately 1 hour.

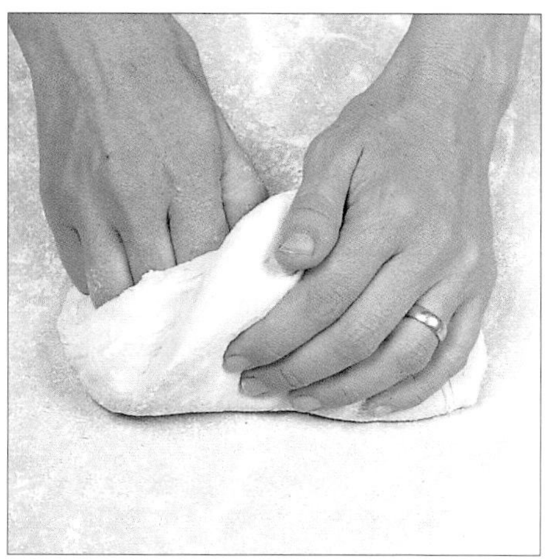

4 Prepare topping for pizza by slicing tomatoes and placing in a pan with juice and tomato paste. Add garlic, herbs, sugar and seasoning. Simmer for 5–10 minutes, with the lid off to allow mixture to reduce. Cool.

5 Knock down proven dough for 1 minute on a lightly floured surface. Roll out into a large circle with a diameter of approximately 35 cm (14 in), or into two smaller circles.

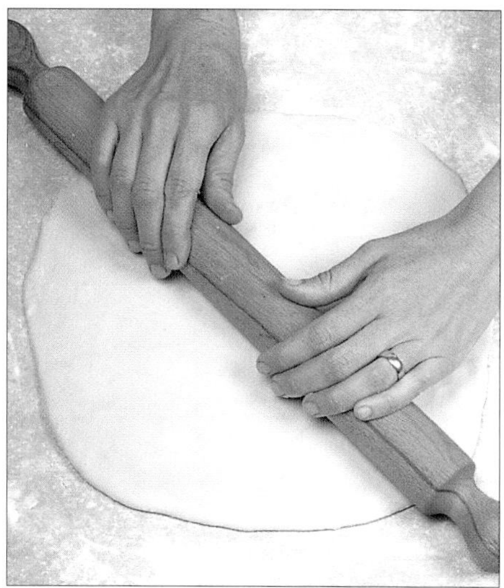

6 Spread pizza base with cooled tomato mixture. Sprinkle with grated mozzarella cheese, followed by toppings of your choice.

7 Finally, sprinkle with grated Parmesan cheese. Bake at 220 °C (425 °F/gas 7) for about 15 minutes. Serve immediately.
SERVES 4.

OLIVE BREAD

A delicious, crusty loaf with the tang of olives.

750 g (1¾ lb) white bread flour
1 tbsp instant yeast
200 ml (7 fl oz) olive oil
4 tbsp oil drained off sun-dried tomatoes (if not using sun-dried tomatoes, replace with olive oil)
2–3 tsp salt
1 tsp freshly ground black pepper
500 ml (17 fl oz) warm water
20 Calamata olives, stoned and finely sliced
50 g (2 oz) finely sliced, sun-dried tomatoes (optional)
2 tbsp olive oil
coarse salt to sprinkle over top of loaf

1 Sift flour into a large bowl. Make a well in the centre, add yeast, and stir to combine.

2 Add oils, salt, pepper and warm water. Mix to a dough.

3 Turn out onto a floured surface and knead for 10 minutes.

4 Place in an oiled bowl, cover loosely with a clean cloth, and put in a warm place to rise until doubled in size. This will take approximately 1 hour.

5 Knock down dough and knead on a lightly floured surface. Roll into a large rectangle. Spread with olive and sun-dried tomato slices, if using. Roll up like a Swiss roll. Knead into a roundish shape.

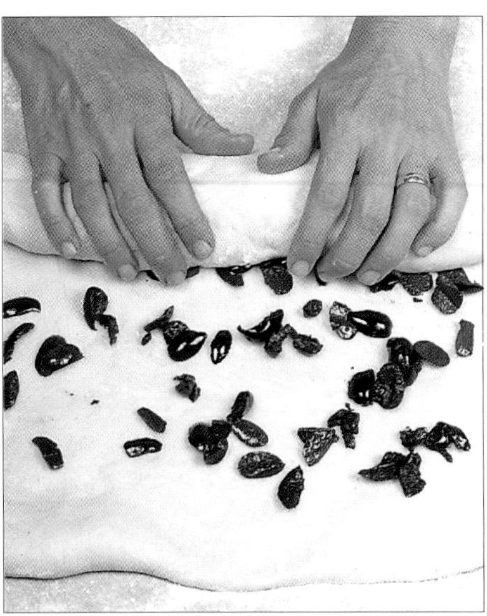

6 Place dough in a 20 cm (8 in) deep x 22 cm (8½ in) wide, cast-iron pan, and spoon the extra 2 tbsp olive oil over dough.

7 Push down dough and turn a couple of times to cover with oil. Sprinkle with coarse salt and set aside in a warm place for 20–30 minutes.

8 Bake at 220 °C (425 °F/gas 7) for 30–40 minutes. Remove from the oven, cool in the pan for 10 minutes, and then serve.
MAKES 1 LARGE LOAF, SUFFICIENT TO FEED 10–12 PEOPLE.

TIPS

- According to your taste, extra slices of sun-dried tomatoes may replace the olives, or vice versa.

- To make a Baguette, follow instructions up to step 5 where dough is rolled into Swiss roll shape. Brush with olive oil and sprinkle with coarse salt. Place on an ungreased baking sheet, cover with a cloth and leave in a warm place for 20 minutes to rise. Bake in oven at 200 °C (400 °F/gas 6) for 30 minutes. The baguette is cooked when it sounds hollow when tapped. Cool on the baking sheet for 5 minutes, and then remove to a rack to cool completely.

GARLIC CHILLI RING

Two favourite flavours combine to make an interesting bread.

1 tbsp instant yeast
575 g (1¼ lb) white bread flour
2 tsp sugar
1–2 finely shredded chillies, or 1 tsp chilli powder
2 tsp garlic salt
2 large eggs, beaten
3 tbsp oil
approximately 500 ml (17 fl oz) lukewarm water

GARLIC CHILLI DIP
200 g (7 oz) butter
2–3 tsp chilli powder
2 cloves garlic, crushed
1 tsp garlic salt
5 tsp chopped fresh parsley

1 In a large mixing bowl, combine yeast, flour, sugar, chillies and garlic salt with a wooden spoon.

2 Combine eggs and oil with 250 ml (8 fl oz) lukewarm water. Add to flour and mix. Add enough water to make a softish dough – it may not need all the water, or it may require a little more.

3 Place dough on a floured surface and knead for about 5–10 minutes. Place in a floured bowl, cover and leave to rise until doubled in size. This will take approximately 1 hour.

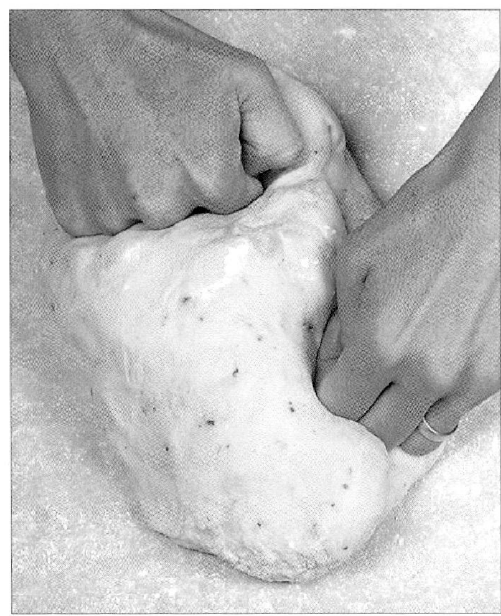

4 Divide the dough in half, and then each half into 12 balls.

5 To make the Garlic Chilli Dip, combine the butter, chilli powder, garlic, garlic salt and fresh parsley. Dunk each ball of dough into the dip to coat well.

6 Place dough balls slightly apart in two 23 cm (9 in) loose-bottomed tins – there should be 12 balls per tin. Cover, and leave to rise for 20 minutes.

7 Place tin on baking sheet and bake at 190 °C (375 °F/gas 5) for 30–35 minutes if baking one tin at a time; if baking both tins together, increase baking time by 5–10 minutes. Remove from oven, cool in tin for 5 minutes, then turn out onto a wire rack to cool.
MAKES 2 RINGS, OR 24 ROLLS.

TIP

◆ The garlic or chilli flavouring can be omitted, if preferred.

WHITE AND BROWN BREAD

Nothing beats the homemade brand!

WHITE BREAD
500 g (11 oz) white bread flour
2 tsp salt
1 tbsp instant yeast
1 tsp sugar
250 ml (8 fl oz) milk
3 tbsp butter
1 large egg, beaten
melted butter or margarine to brush over crust

BROWN BREAD
250 g (9 oz) white bread flour
2 tsp salt
250 g (9 oz) wholemeal flour
1 tbsp instant yeast
1 tsp sugar
250 ml (8 fl oz) milk
3 tbsp butter
1 large egg, beaten
cracked wheat to sprinkle over top of loaf

1 To make the white bread, sift flour and salt into a large mixing bowl. For brown loaf, sift together white bread flour and salt, then stir in wholemeal flour. For both loaves, continue as follows: stir in instant yeast and sugar.

2 Warm milk and melt butter in the milk. Cool to blood temperature. Add beaten egg to milk mixture.

3 Pour onto flour mixture and mix to a softish dough, adding more warmed milk if necessary. Knead on a lightly floured surface for 5 minutes.

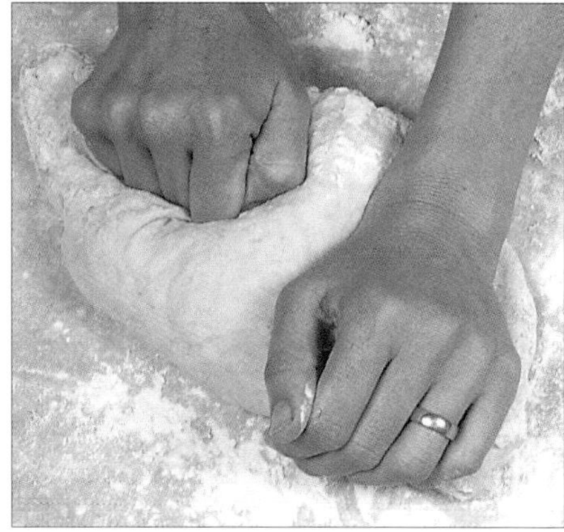

4 Place dough in a lightly floured or oiled bowl, and leave to rise for approximately 1 hour, until doubled in size.

5 Lightly knock down dough, and roll into large rectangle. Then roll up like a Swiss roll, to get an even-shaped loaf.

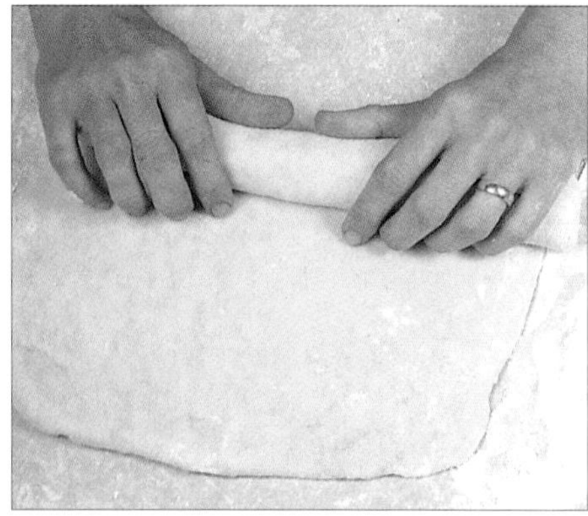

6 Place in an 8 x 23 cm (3 x 9 in) large loaf tin. Cover and put in a warm place to rise until dough reaches the top of the tin.

7 To make the crust for brown bread, brush the top of the dough with water and sprinkle with cracked wheat just before baking. Bake the loaves at 220 °C (425 °F/gas 7) for 30 minutes. Remove from the oven and cool in the tin for 5 minutes, then turn out to cool on a rack. To make a crust with a glow for the white bread, brush with melted butter or margarine while still warm after baking.
MAKES 1 WHITE AND 1 BROWN LOAF.

TIP

◆ The basic white bread dough can be used to make a variety of shaped loaves, e.g. round or plaited loaves, or rolls.

CANDIED POPCORN BALLS

Popcorn is all the rage. These balls are unusual, easy to make, and the perfect treat for a children's party.

6 x 250 ml (8 fl oz) popped popcorn
75 g (3 oz) seedless raisins
75 g (3 oz) sultanas
500 ml (17 fl oz) water
200 g (7 oz) white sugar
2 tbsp butter
pinch of salt
2 tsp food colouring of your choice

1 Spray a large mixing bowl with non-stick cooking spray. Combine popcorn, raisins and sultanas in the bowl.

2 Combine water, sugar, butter, salt and food colouring in a heavy-based saucepan. Stir over low heat until sugar has dissolved, and then bring to the boil.

3 Place a lid on the saucepan and boil for 2 minutes. Remove lid and boil for further 30 minutes. Do not stir as stirring can cause crystallization.

4 When it reaches the 'hard ball' stage (a teaspoonful of syrup dropped into cold water will form a hard ball), it is ready to pour over the popcorn mixture.

5 Pour syrup over the popcorn mixture and stir thoroughly. Working very quickly, rub hands with butter or non-stick cooking spray, then form mixture into small balls. Place on greased baking sheet, and allow to cool and set.
MAKES 12–18 BALLS.

TIPS

◆ To make candied popcorn, simply leave the popcorn after stirring in the syrup in step 5 and do not form it into balls.

◆ Push wooden skewers into the popcorn balls while still warm, to make popcorn sticks.

◆ Replace sultanas with sunflower seeds for more crunch.

◆ Popcorn is a healthy snack because of its high fibre and fairly low fat and salt content.

◆ To make popcorn, pre-heat 1 tbsp oil in a heavy-based saucepan with a lid. Cover bottom of the pan with a single layer of popcorn. Replace lid and cook over high heat, shaking to distribute the kernels and allow them all to pop. Be careful not to burn. Remove pan from the heat once the popping has stopped. Salt lightly and, if desired, pour melted butter over the popcorn.

◆ To stop popcorn sticking to your hands in step 5, dip hands into cold water before forming balls. Repeat as necessary.

TURKISH DELIGHT

3 tbsp gelatine
85 ml (3 fl oz) water
200 ml (7 fl oz) water
500 g (18 oz) caster sugar
½ tsp tartaric acid
2 tsp rose water
few drops of pink food colouring
sifted icing sugar

1 Sprinkle gelatine over 85 ml (3 fl oz) water in a bowl. Leave to sponge.

2 Pour 200 ml (7 fl oz) water into a heavy-based saucepan. Add sugar, and stir over low heat until dissolved.

3 Soften the gelatine sponge in the microwave on Medium for 2 minutes, or place over a pan of boiling water, off the cooker, until softened. Add the gelatine and tartaric acid to the sugar syrup. Simmer for 5 minutes.

4 Remove the saucepan from the heat, and add the rose water and the pink colouring. Lightly oil an 18 cm (7 in) square tin, or prepare by spraying the tin with a non-stick cooking spray. Pour the mixture into the tin, and leave to set.

5 When set, cut into cubes and toss in icing sugar. Store in an airtight container dredged with extra icing sugar.

MAKES APPROXIMATELY 18 CUBES.

TIPS

◆ Rose water is available from a pharmacy.

◆ To make green Turkish Delight, replace the pink food colouring with green colouring.

◆ Add a few drops of peppermint oil for a mint flavour.

◆ To make a nutty Turkish Delight, add 100 g (4 oz) toasted and chopped almonds, pine nuts or pistachios with the rose water and the food colouring in step 4.

◆ Turkish Delight makes a perfect gift. To present it beautifully, simply place a sheet of clear cellophane inside a decorative box or container, and neatly fill with Turkish Delight. Tie up the bundle with a pretty ribbon.

FUDGE

Fudge is always a favourite. This simple recipe works well; for a larger quantity, simply double up.

500 g (18 oz) white sugar
1 x 397 g can full cream condensed milk
4 tbsp butter
150 ml (5 fl oz) water
2 tsp vanilla essence

1 In a heavy-based, deep saucepan combine sugar, condensed milk, butter and water.

2 Stir constantly until all the sugar has melted. Wash down the sides of the pan with a pastry brush dipped in water to remove sugar crystals. Bring mixture to the boil. Boil for 30–40 minutes, stirring occasionally so that mixture does not catch at the bottom.

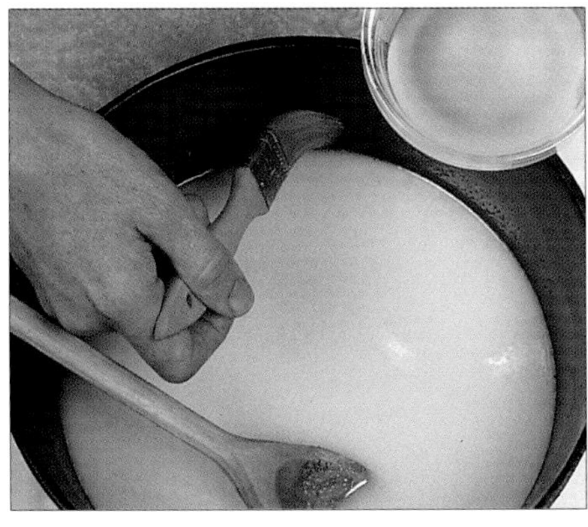

3 The fudge will be ready when it has changed into a typical caramel fudge colour, and has reached the 'soft ball' stage (a teaspoonful of mixture dropped into cold water will form a soft ball).

4 Add vanilla essence. Remove from heat and beat vigorously with a wooden spoon. Mixture will thicken and become grainy.

5 Pour into a greased 18 x 28 cm (7 x 11 in) baking tin. Cut into squares before completely cool, then leave in the tin to set.
MAKES APPROXIMATELY 24–36 PIECES.

TIPS

◆ For a nutty fudge, add 100 g (4 oz) roasted and chopped nuts of your choice to the mixture, just before beating with a wooden spoon in step 4.

◆ For successful sweet-making, follow these general rules:
- Use a heavy-based saucepan.
- Use good-quality white granulated sugar.
- Mix all ingredients very well before boiling.
- Stir over low heat until all the sugar dissolves, washing the sugar crystals down with a pastry brush dipped in water.
- Do not stir once the mixture has come to the boil, as stirring can cause the sugar mixture to crystallize.

◆ A sugar thermometer is very useful. Buy one from a speciality kitchenware shop.

◆ Condensed milk is made from full cream milk which is heated until half the water content has evaporated; sugar is added as a preservative. To reconstitute condensed milk, add an equal measure of water, but use this only in sweet dishes as it will still be very sweet.

TOFFEE APPLES

6 large red apples
6 kebab sticks

TOFFEE
600 g (1lb 5 oz) granulated sugar
375 ml (13 fl oz) water
$1/2$ tsp cream of tartar
1 tsp red or green food colouring

1 Remove stalks from apples. Wash apples in mild soapy solution – this helps the syrup to stick to them – and dry thoroughly. Insert a stick into each apple.

2 To make toffee, butter the top 5 cm (2 in) of a heavy-based 3 litre ($5^1/_4$ pint) saucepan. Add sugar to the pan and dissolve in water over low heat, stirring constantly. Wash sugar crystals off the side of the pan with a pastry brush dipped in water. Add cream of tartar.

3 Bring the toffee mixture to the boil, cover, and boil for 3 minutes. Remove the lid, and continue boiling until the syrup changes to a caramel colour. This can take 20–30 minutes. Remove from the heat.

4 Add the food colouring and then mix. To do this, hold the saucepan by the handles and swirl around with your hands – do not stir the toffee. Leave the toffee to stand for a minute before coating the apples.

5 Working carefully, as the toffee is extremely hot, dip the apples into toffee, twirling to cover completely. Dunk very quickly into cold water, spin around to dry, and place on a greased baking sheet.
MAKES 6 TOFFEE APPLES.

TIPS

- To make individual toffees, pour any remaining toffee into a greased tin and, while still warm, cut into squares.
- Toffee apples are hot favourites at cake and sweet stalls at fêtes. The better looking the item, the better it will sell, so wrap toffee apples in brightly coloured cellophane and decorate with pretty ribbons for brisk sales.
- This toffee recipe may easily be doubled.
- Don't make toffee apples on very wet and rainy days: the sugar attracts water and the toffee becomes even stickier than usual.

MARSHMALLOWS

300 g (11 oz) sugar
pinch of salt
1 tbsp golden syrup
250 ml (8 fl oz) water
2 tbsp gelatine
100 ml (3½ fl oz) water
2 extra-large egg whites
1 tsp vanilla essence
125 g (4½ oz) desiccated coconut

1 Butter the top 5 cm (2 in) of a heavy-based saucepan. Dissolve sugar, salt and syrup in 250 ml (8 fl oz) water, stirring constantly. Do not allow the mixture to boil until the sugar has dissolved. Wash sugar crystals off the side of the pot with a pastry brush dipped in water. Cover, and bring to the boil for 3 minutes, and then uncover pan.

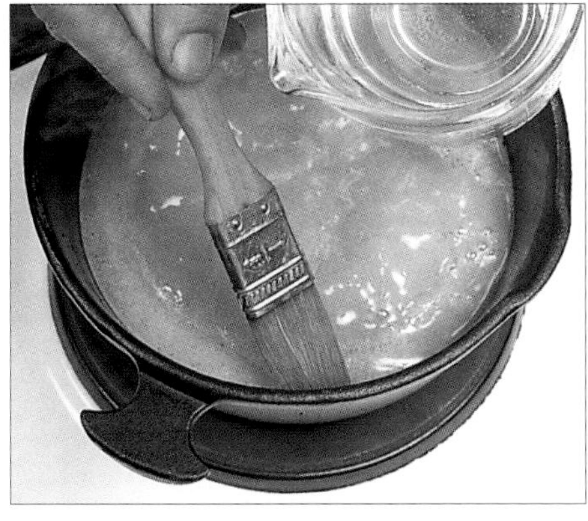

2 Boil until the 'soft-ball' stage is reached (a teaspoonful of mixture dropped into cold water will form a soft ball). Remove from the heat.

3 Meanwhile, dissolve the gelatine in 100 ml (3½ fl oz) water, and allow to form a sponge. Then dissolve the gelatine sponge in the sugar syrup.

4 Stiffly beat egg whites in bowl of electric mixer. Gradually pour hot syrup onto stiffly beaten egg whites, and continue beating until mixture holds its shape. This will take approximately 5 minutes. Beat in vanilla essence.

5 Pour into a greased 20 cm (8 in) square tin. Cover and leave to set in the refrigerator.

6 If desired, toast the coconut in a heavy frying pan. Stir constantly with a wooden spoon over a medium heat, until the coconut is golden brown.

7 Dip a sharp knife into boiling water and cut marshmallows into squares. Roll squares in cooled toasted coconut, or plain desiccated coconut. If preferred plain, simply roll in sifted icing sugar.

MAKES ABOUT 24 MARSHMALLOWS.

TIP

◆ For pink marshmallows, add 1 tsp pink food colouring to the beaten egg whites in step 4.

INDEX